ALSO BY JAMES RISEN

The Main Enemy:
The Inside Story of the CIA's Final Showdown with the KBG
(co-authored with Milt Bearden)

Wrath of Angels:
The American Abortion War
(co-authored with Judy Thomas)

STATE

OF **WAR**

THE SECRET HISTORY

OF THE CIA AND THE

BUSH ADMINISTRATION

James Risen

FREE PRESS   NEW YORK • LONDON • TORONTO • SYDNEY

_f_**P**

FREE PRESS
A Division of Simon & Schuster, Inc.
1230 Avenue of the Americas
New York, NY 10020

FREE PRESS and colophon are trademarks
of Simon & Schuster, Inc.

Designed by Dana Sloan

Manufactured in the United States of America

10   9   8   7   6   5   4   3   2   1

Library of Congress Cataloging-in-Publication Data is available.

ISBN-13: 978-0-7432-7066-3
ISBN-10:   0-7432-7066-5

For information regarding special discounts for bulk purchases,
please contact Simon & Schuster Special Sales at 1-800-456-6798
or business@simonandschuster.com

To Penny

CONTENTS

A NOTE ON SOURCES

Many people have criticized the use of anonymous sources of late. Yet all reporters know that the very best stories—the most important, the most sensitive—rely on them. This book would not be possible without the cooperation of many current and former officials from the Bush administration, the intelligence community, and other parts of the government. Many of them were willing to discuss sensitive matters only on the condition of anonymity.

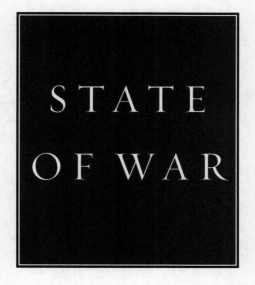

STATE
OF WAR

Prologue
THE SECRET HISTORY

PRESIDENT GEORGE W. BUSH angrily hung up the telephone, emphatically ending a tense conversation with his father, the former president of the United States, George Herbert Walker Bush.

It was 2003, and the argument between the forty-first and forty-third presidents of the United States was the culmination of a prolonged, if very secret, period of friction between the father and son. While the exact details of the conversation are known only to the two men, several highly placed sources say that the argument was related to the misgivings Bush's father felt at the time about the way in which George W. Bush was running his administration. George Herbert Walker Bush was disturbed that his son was allowing Secretary of Defense Donald Rumsfeld and a cadre of neoconservative ideologues to exert broad influence over foreign policy, particularly concerning Iraq, and that he seemed to be tuning out the advice of moderates, including Secretary of State Colin Powell. In other words, George Bush's own father privately shared some of the same concerns that were being voiced at the time by his son's public critics.

Later, the president called his father back and apologized for hanging up on him, and no permanent rift developed, according to sources familiar with the incident.

Yet the father-son argument underscores the degree to which the presidency of George W. Bush has marked a radical departure from

1

the centrist traditions of U.S. foreign policy, embodied by his father. Since World War Two, foreign policy and national security have been areas in which American presidents of both parties have tended toward cautious pragmatism. On issues of war and peace, both liberal Democrats and conservative Republicans have in the past recognized that the stakes were too high to risk sudden and impetuous actions based on politics or ideology. Even presidents with strong visions of America's place in the world—Ronald Reagan, John F. Kennedy—moved slowly and deliberately before taking actions that might place American soldiers in harm's way. The United States was supposed to be slow to anger.

George Herbert Walker Bush grew up within that tradition and embraced it as president. When he went to war against Iraq in 1991, he did so only after Saddam Hussein invaded neighboring Kuwait, and only after gaining the broad support of an international coalition. After liberating Kuwait—the sole stated objective of that war—the elder Bush halted American troops rather than march toward Baghdad to topple Saddam.

George W. Bush was elected by voters who expected a repeat of the presidency of George Herbert Walker Bush. He reinforced that belief when he said, at a campaign debate in October 2000, that he planned to pursue a "humble" foreign policy: "If we're an arrogant nation, they'll resent us; if we're a humble nation, but strong, they'll welcome us."

But after 9/11, George W. Bush parted ways with the traditions of his father, and that decision has had consequences that are still playing themselves out. Above all, it has led to a disturbing breakdown of the checks and balances within the executive branch of the United States government. Among the consequences: a new domestic spying program, a narco-state in Afghanistan, and chaos in Iraq.

* * *

The National Security Council (NSC) at the White House, created during the Cold War to manage the enormous military, intelligence, and foreign policy apparatus of the U.S. government, has been weak and dysfunctional in the Bush administration, according to many officials who have served in the administration. As national security advisor during Bush's first term, Condoleezza Rice had an excellent personal relationship with the president but lacked sufficient power and authority to get crucial things done. Foreign policy was often forged by small groups in unlikely places, including the Office of the Vice President and the Office of the Secretary of Defense. Rice was forced to play catch-up and to accept professional indignities, particularly at the hands of Donald Rumsfeld. Some of her chagrined aides believe others in her place would have resigned. Her loyalty was rewarded, however, when Bush named her Secretary of State at the start of his second term.

In many cases, policies weren't debated at all. There never was a formal meeting of all of the president's senior advisors to debate and decide whether to invade Iraq, according to a senior administration source. And the most fateful decision of the postinvasion period—the move by American proconsul L. Paul Bremer to disband the Iraqi army—may have been made without President Bush's advance knowledge, according to a senior White House source. The well-placed source said he is virtually certain that the president did not know of the decision before it was taken. The action, almost certainly coordinated with Rumsfeld, contradicted the recommendations of an interagency planning group chaired by the National Security Council.

The absence of effective management has been the defining characteristic of the Bush administration's foreign policy and has allowed radical decisions to take effect rapidly with minimal review.

* * *

The ease with which the Bush administration has been able to over-
come bureaucratic resistance throughout the government has revealed the weaknesses of both the military's officer corps and the
nation's intelligence community. In very different ways, the army
and the Central Intelligence Agency (CIA) have traditionally served
as gravitational forces supporting the status quo. Dominated by career professionals, both institutions abhor sudden change and tend to
force policy toward the middle.

But under Bush, the army and the CIA have failed to put up
much of a bureaucratic fight, despite deep anger and frustration
within their ranks over the administration's conduct of national security policy. The docility of the American officer corps is particularly striking. One senior administration source notes that during his
visits to Iraq, he invariably heard American commanders complain
about such problems as the lack of sufficient troops. But during
meetings and videoconferences with Bush and Rumsfeld in which
this source participated, those same senior military commanders
would not voice their complaints. Their silence in the face of authority allowed the White House to state publicly that U.S. commanders
in the field were satisfied with the resources at their disposal and that
they had never requested additional troops for Iraq.

No other institution failed in its mission as completely during the
Bush years as did the CIA. It was already deeply troubled by the time
he took office in 2001 (as one rogue operation from 2000, recounted
here, attests). By the end of Bush's first term, the CIA looked like the
government's equivalent of Enron, an organization whose bank-
ruptcy triggered cries for reform.

It takes only a little more than one decade's worth of history to
understand how the CIA found itself, in the period before the 2003
invasion of Iraq, producing what amounted to White House talking
points rather than independent and disciplined intelligence reports.

The roots of the CIA's corruption can be traced back to the end of the Cold War.

When the Soviet Union collapsed in 1991, the CIA's original mission ended. The agency had been created in 1947 for a singular purpose, to wage war against Soviet Communism, and for generations of CIA officers all other issues had been secondary.

The post–Cold War era dawned with critics charging that the CIA had overstated the Soviet threat and questioning whether an agency that had been surprised by the fall of the Berlin Wall had become obsolete. The Clinton administration and Congress soon began slashing the intelligence budget in search of a peace dividend, and Bill Clinton showed almost no interest in intelligence matters. His first CIA director, James Woolsey, felt so isolated from the president and the rest of the administration that he lasted barely two years.

In the midst of this public reassessment of the agency's role in the new era, CIA officer Aldrich Ames was arrested as a Russian spy in 1994, triggering an acrimonious period of mole hunting and finger pointing and setting the agency further back on its heels. Senior CIA officers began heading for the exits en masse. Over a three- or four-year period in the early to mid-1990s, virtually an entire generation of CIA officers—the people who had won the Cold War—quit or retired. One CIA veteran compared the agency to an airline that had lost all of its senior pilots.

The brief but bitter tenure of CIA director John M. Deutch only hastened the agency's fall. When he arrived at the CIA in 1995, Deutch made no secret of the fact that he didn't want the job and that he had only accepted the post in the belief that President Clinton would later reward him by naming him secretary of defense. Unable to mask his dislike for the CIA, he quickly alienated a crucial constituency—the Directorate of Operations (DO), the agency's clandestine service. His decision to fire senior officers over a scandal in Guatemala may have been sound management practice, but it led to an open rebellion within the DO, from which he never fully recovered. Morale plunged to new lows, and the agency became paralyzed by an aversion to high-risk espionage operations for fear they would lead to political flaps. Less willing to take big risks, the CIA was less able to recruit spies in dangerous places such as Iraq.

At the same time, the CIA tried to answer public questions about its post–Cold War mission by taking on a series of new problems, including nuclear proliferation, terrorism, and international narcotics trafficking. There would be new "rogue states" to track—North Korea, Iraq, Iran—and regional conflicts to contain in places such as the former Yugoslavia.

Woolsey liked to say that the CIA had fought a dragon for forty years but now faced lots of poisonous snakes; an array of smaller problems, rather than one big threat. But these were parallel missions. The CIA no longer had a single focus. And it would soon become obvious that the CIA was not particularly good at multitasking.

In the absence of one overriding priority like the Soviet Union, it became much more tempting for CIA management to shift resources from one target to another, depending on the interests and even the whims of the administration in power. Thanks to Vice President Al Gore, for example, the CIA briefly made the global environment one of its priorities.

More broadly, the growth of cable news networks and later the Internet intensified the pressures on policy makers to respond to the crisis of the moment, and policy makers, in turn, pressured the CIA. Sometimes these whims changed daily. Long-term research and in-depth analysis suffered as CIA managers and analysts became fixated on the race to get late-breaking tidbits of intelligence into the President's Daily Brief. To get ahead, analysts learned, they had to master the trick of writing quick, short reports that would grab the attention of top policy makers. CIA analysts had become the classified equivalent of television reporters, rather than college professors. The result was that fewer analysts were taking the time to go back and challenge basic assumptions.

"If I had to point to one specific problem that explains why we are doing such a bad job on intelligence, it is this almost single-minded focus on current reporting," observes Carl Ford, a former CIA analyst and former chief of the Bureau of Intelligence and Research at the State Department. In the 1970s, Ford adds, 70 percent to 80 percent of CIA analysts spent their time doing basic research on key topics; today, about 90 percent of analysts do nothing but current reporting. "Analysts today are looking at intelligence coming in and then writing what they think about it, but they have no depth of knowledge to determine whether the current intelligence is correct. There are very few people left in the intelligence community who even remember how to do basic research."

George Tenet walked into this dangerous mix when he became Deutch's accidental successor in 1997. When Deutch resigned at the end of 1996, Clinton's first choice to take over at the CIA was Tony Lake, his national security advisor during his first term. But Lake's nomination succumbed to the Republican-controlled Senate, where he was considered too liberal and too close to Clinton. After Lake withdrew, Clinton turned to Tenet almost by default. Tenet had been serving as Deutch's deputy, had earlier worked on intelligence policy at the White House, and before that had served as staff director of the U.S. Senate Select Committee on Intelligence. His time on Capitol Hill meant that he had the most important asset that Clinton was looking for at the time: George Tenet was confirmable.

In the space of just a few years, Tenet's career had soared from Senate staffer to leader of the American intelligence community, and he was determined not to repeat the mistakes of his predecessors. Woolsey had failed because he had no relationship with the president; Deutch had failed because he alienated the clandestine service. Tenet would devote himself to courting the Oval Office and the Directorate of Operations.

In many ways, Tenet was a fine peacetime DCI. He worked hard to rebuild the shattered morale of the CIA while lobbying Congress and the White House to increase the agency's budget. He dispelled the poisonous climate of the Deutch years and won plaudits by bringing back a legendary Cold Warrior, Jack G. Downing, to run the Directorate of Operations in a bid to return the DO to its espionage roots.

But as one former CIA officer noted, Tenet was a great cheerleader, not a great leader, and while he rebuilt budgets and morale, the structural weaknesses of the U.S. intelligence community were not addressed. The failure to deal with hard management problems during peacetime would come back to haunt Tenet when a new administration, one with a harder edge and a much greater interest in intelligence, came into office.

In hindsight, even many of Tenet's admirers and associates believe he should have quit the CIA when Bill Clinton left office. He could have left with his reputation untainted by 9/11 and the hunt for Iraqi weapons of mass destruction (WMD) and would have been remembered as the man who turned the CIA around. Tenet might also be remembered for the displays of refreshing bluntness that he exhibited early in his time at the CIA, even at a personal cost.

When, for instance, President Clinton considered commuting the sentence of convicted Israeli spy Jonathan Pollard in order to win Israeli concessions in the Middle East peace negotiations, Tenet told Clinton he would quit if Pollard were released. Clinton backed down. And in May 1998, when the CIA was caught by surprise by India's testing of a nuclear bomb, Tenet had to deal with the consequences of the first major intelligence failure to occur on his watch. As soon as the news broke, Tenet talked by phone with Senator Richard C. Shelby, the wily Alabama Republican who was the chairman of the Senate Select Committee on Intelligence.

"George, what happened?" Shelby asked.

"Senator," Tenet replied, "we didn't have a clue."

Tenet's blunt comment deeply troubled Shelby, and the senator would later say that it was that conversation that marked the start of his concerns about Tenet's management of the CIA. Shelby would later emerge as Tenet's most vocal critic.

Tenet's comments were painfully honest. In later years, in fact, "We don't have a clue," or words to that effect, might have served George Tenet well.

Throughout the Bush years, the United States has confronted what amounts to an ill-formed yet global Sunni Muslim insurgency, one that has evolved and expanded far beyond the original al Qaeda terrorist network that attacked New York and Washington on September 11, 2001. In Iraq, Afghanistan, Europe, the Middle East, and southeast Asia, Islamist terrorism has been growing ever more deadly.

The fundamental political question facing Washington is whether or not President Bush's policies have made terrorism worse, by failing to deliver a knockout blow to al Qaeda when he had the chance, and by subsequently deepening the antagonism toward the United States within the Sunni Arab world with his handling of Iraq. It is becoming painfully clear that the number of young Muslims willing to strap on explosives is growing faster than the ability of the United States and its allies to capture and kill them. It sometimes seems as if the Bush administration is fighting the birthrate of the entire Arab world.

Bush's supporters rightly point to a new yearning for democratic reform that has begun to sweep through the Middle East. President Bush certainly deserves credit for making the spread of democracy a centerpiece of his agenda. Eventually, the president's ambitious dream may turn out to be right—perhaps the war in Iraq will turn out to have been the event that broke the decades-long political stagnation in the Arab world. Perhaps that, in turn, will lead to progress in Arab-Israeli relations and a broader sense of hopefulness that will compete with extremism and terror.

In effect, Bush has taken an enormous gamble with American policy in the Arab world—and with the lives of American soldiers. He has placed a bet that the popular desire for democracy triggered by the toppling of Saddam Hussein will outpace the rise of Islamic extremism, which has been stoked in part by that same American invasion of Iraq. Bush has unleashed so many competing forces in the Middle East that no one can safely predict the outcome.

These questions may not be answered for years, and they may provide history's ultimate judgment of George W. Bush. Some of the short-term effects of his presidency, however, are now coming into view.

Underneath that broad arc of global events, there is a secret history of the CIA and the Bush administration both before and especially after 9/11. It is a cautionary tale, one that shows how the most covert tools of American national security policy have been misused. It involves domestic spying, abuse of power, and outrageous operations. It is a tale that can only now begin to be told.

1

"WHO AUTHORIZED PUTTING HIM ON PAIN MEDICATION?"

B Y THE EARLY SPRING of 2002, George Tenet had developed an extraordinarily close and complicated relationship with George W. Bush, perhaps the nearest thing to a genuine friendship that has ever developed between a CIA director and the president he served. It was a relationship in which George Tenet started out as the aggressive suitor, but the imbalance in power between the two men inevitably meant that Tenet ended up as the one seduced.

Bush found in Tenet not just a fellow jock—Tenet is a true expert on college basketball and an ardent fan of Georgetown University, his alma mater—but a streetwise, tough-talking Greek kid from Queens, an image enhanced by his nasty habit of swilling chopped cigars around his mouth as he speaks. Tenet struck a chord with a president who once owned the Texas Rangers and who revels in jocular banter. The president prizes plain speaking above almost all else; Tenet gave it to him. Unlike Bush, Tenet was overweight and in poor physical shape, and suffered heart problems at an early age during the Clinton years. Still, Tenet was a gruff battler, spending time exer-

11

cising and playing pickup basketball with other CIA employees, which had to appeal to the fitness freak in Bush.

As a successful former Senate and White House staffer, Tenet was a master at managing individual relationships with older and more powerful men. Finding ways to please one powerful man was the path to success in the hothouse culture of Capitol Hill. Tenet had also transferred to Washington an ethnic Greek sense of the importance of relationships. For Tenet, public policy could always be broken down into a series of personal transactions.

At the same time, at least a few who worked closely with Tenet didn't necessarily believe that his ability to co-opt powerful men was a good thing, and it was a trait that eventually wore out its welcome. By the end of the Clinton years, Tenet was quite popular with the CIA rank and file; he was seen as the man who had led them out of the wilderness of the bleak Deutch years. He also engendered fierce and lasting loyalty among some of his top lieutenants. Yet there were at least a few at the CIA and the White House who had gradually discovered another side to Tenet's personality. In public, Tenet struck a pose as an honest broker of intelligence; in private, he was sometimes seen as someone who would tell people what they wanted to hear but would later say the opposite to others. At least a few insiders at the CIA and White House found it frustrating whenever they tried to get a fix on him. Tenet seemed to these insiders to be extremely adaptable, and while that was to be expected in a politician, it was a little bit unsettling in the man charged with running the U.S. intelligence community.

Some of Tenet's aides were convinced that if Al Gore won the election, Tenet would not be one of the Clinton people kept on in the new Gore administration. But Al Gore did not win, so to keep his job, all Tenet had to do was to make a good first impression on one man, George W. Bush, and he was a master at that. For Tenet, managing George Bush was not that much different from managing Senator David Boren, Tony Lake, or John Deutch, Tenet's previous bosses. First, you find out what they want, and then you make sure you are the one who gives it to them.

Longtime Tenet watchers knew that if he had enough time alone with Bush, he would win him over. At the CIA, the word soon spread that Tenet had "case officered" the new president, a high compliment within the spy world. Bush even tagged Tenet with an insider nickname—"Jorge"—a sign that the rumpled and affable CIA director had been accepted at the Bush White House.

Yet Tenet only narrowly survived the Clinton-Bush transition. In fact, Bush had nearly dumped Tenet, who was initially seen among Bush aides as a Clinton holdover with no particular political standing. He was kept on only at the last minute, only when Bush's father urged his son to do so, and only when there was no other obvious candidate to fill the job. The Bush transition team had at first envisioned Donald Rumsfeld as the new director of central intelligence. Dick Cheney's old mentor during the Nixon and Ford days, Rumsfeld had recently chaired two commissions: one on the ballistic missile threat facing the United States and the other on the military and intelligence uses of space. Both panels had become deeply involved in reviewing the performance of the intelligence community during the 1990s. Rumsfeld came away from those commissions convinced that the CIA was broken, and he seemed intrigued by the job of fixing it.

But the Pentagon opened up instead. After a personal meeting, Bush had soured on the leading candidate for secretary of defense, former Senator Dan Coats of Indiana. Suddenly, the idea of having Rumsfeld, a headstrong executive with few doubts about his own managerial abilities, return to the job that he had held briefly during the Ford administration, seemed appealing, both to Cheney and Rumsfeld. Some Bush administration officials believed that Cheney wanted a strong figure like Rumsfeld at the Pentagon to provide a counterbalance to the power and influence he expected to be exerted by Colin Powell, who was poised to become secretary of state. Richard Armitage, a close friend of Powell's, had been slated to be

Coats's number two at Defense, and the idea of having Powell at State and Armitage at the Pentagon seemed to worry Cheney. He feared that Powell and his camp would have the whole administration wired. Armitage ended up as Powell's deputy at State instead.

Shifting Rumsfeld to the Pentagon meant that the CIA post was still up in the air. But even with Rumsfeld out of the picture, Tenet still didn't have a lock on keeping his job, at least in part because of the man handling intelligence issues for the Bush transition team. Richard Haver, a former naval intelligence officer with strong Republican ties—he had worked as Cheney's intelligence aide at the Pentagon in the first Bush administration—was running the CIA transition team for the younger Bush, and he was no fan of George Tenet. During the transition, Haver made it clear to Cheney that he believed that the new administration should get rid of Tenet. Haver had built his reputation as a key player in some of the navy's riskiest and most secretive Cold War intelligence operations, most notably the use of submarines to tap into Soviet navy communications cables off the Soviet Union's coast, and he had become a leading critic of Tenet and the culture of risk aversion that he believed Tenet had allowed to fester at the post–Cold War CIA. Haver believed Tenet was too weak and too political to be DCI.

For Haver, Tenet was the embodiment of everything wrong with the Clinton administration's feckless and misguided approach to national security. Other leading Republicans agreed. Senator Richard Shelby, the Alabama Republican who was chairman of the Senate Intelligence Committee at the time, had developed into a painfully public critic of Tenet, and he couldn't help wondering why Bush was even considering keeping Tenet on. Bush never asked Shelby for his advice on the matter, however.

A number of CIA officials believed that Haver was not an impartial observer and that he was interested in the job for himself. That was a prospect that many at the CIA dreaded, since his dislike for the agency was well known and went far beyond his personal distaste for

George Tenet. As an outsider to the CIA culture, Haver had been brought in to lead the agency's damage assessment of the Aldrich Ames spy case, and he had spared no one in his scathing criticism of the way in which the CIA allowed Ames to operate freely for the nine years prior to the Soviet mole's 1994 arrest.

When Haver told Cheney that they should dump Tenet, he phrased his recommendation indirectly. He said that Tenet had been ignored during the Clinton years, and that the Bush administration should not have a DCI who is ignored by the president. Cheney understood his meaning and didn't argue with Haver's assessment of Tenet. But he told Haver that the decision was out of his hands. It was up to the president-elect, and Bush was talking to his father about it.

It now seems clear that George H. W. Bush saved George Tenet's job. George W. Bush's father counseled his son that he should keep the CIA out of the political cycle, that the CIA director's job shouldn't change hands each time a new administration came in. The elder Bush had served as CIA director for one year under Gerald Ford, prior to Ford's defeat in the 1976 election. Bush had then appealed to Jimmy Carter to keep him on at the CIA under the new administration. But Carter had rejected the idea and replaced Bush with his own man, Stansfield Turner. That old slight still rankled with Bush senior, who felt it was important to signal that the CIA was free from politics. That meant keeping Tenet.

"I think it was the father," said one former Tenet aide, referring to Bush Sr.'s role. "I've been told that Bush talked to his father, and his father told him that you have plenty of other things to worry about, and you can leave him there for a while, and that's what he thought Carter should have done for him—take it out of the direct election process. But I don't think he thought he needed to keep him forever."

It also didn't hurt that Tenet had been ingratiating himself with the elder Bush for the last several years, perhaps anticipating a Bush family restoration. He had presided over the 1999 ceremony renaming CIA headquarters the George Bush Center for Intelligence. He had arranged, later that same year, for the CIA to sponsor a Cold War history conference at the George Bush Presidential Library, featuring speakers from the first Bush administration. More quietly, he had also arranged a series of classified intelligence briefings for the former president, including some in Houston, Bush's hometown, during the later stages of the Clinton administration. Former presidents are entitled to such CIA briefings, but some CIA insiders wondered whether the briefings given the elder Bush went beyond the normal practice.

Tenet's allies lobbied for him as well. David Boren, the president of the University of Oklahoma and a former Democratic senator from Oklahoma, who had been the chairman of the Senate Intelligence Committee when Tenet was its staff director, was Tenet's most important mentor. Like both Bushes, Boren was a Yale graduate (Class of 1963) and a member of Skull and Bones, the elitist secret Yale society that George W. Bush (Class of 1968) joined a few years later. Boren was said by other Tenet allies to have strongly recommended Tenet to Bush.

Eli Jacobs, a New York investor and former owner of the Baltimore Orioles, and a kind of high-level CIA groupie, was close friends with Tenet and also knew the Bush family. Jacobs and George W. Bush had been American League team owners at the same time in the early 1990s. Over breakfast in December 1999, Jacobs tried to convince the Texas governor that he and Tenet were a lot alike, that they talked the same and swore the same, and that they would get along if Bush gave Tenet a chance.

During the abbreviated transition, Tenet's personal intelligence briefings for the president-elect went well, and the younger Bush seemed impressed. Finally, at the end of one briefing in mid-January 2001, just before the inauguration, Bush asked everyone except Tenet to leave the room. Alone, he told Tenet he would like him to stay on as CIA director, at least for a while. He would decide later how their relationship was developing. Bush added that he hoped it would work out.

Within the Bush transition team, this decision was seen as something of a setback for Cheney and his conservative foreign policy camp, which was still coalescing around the vice president's office and had not yet turned the Pentagon into a sanctuary. Days later, Haver ran into Eli Jacobs in Washington and admitted defeat. "Congratulations, you guys won." Instead of CIA director, Haver became Rumsfeld's special assistant on intelligence at the Pentagon, the same job he had held under Cheney a decade earlier. Haver's presence in the Office of the Secretary of Defense did not bode well for the future of Pentagon-CIA relations.

When Bush decided to keep Tenet, he made his decision public in the most offhand way possible. Four days before Bush's inauguration, Ari Fleischer, the transition spokesman who was about to become White House press secretary, simply told a reporter in response to a question in a press briefing that Tenet was staying at the CIA for the foreseeable future. "Director Tenet has been asked to stay on the job for what will amount to an undetermined period of time," Fleischer said, "but he has been asked to stay on." Bush made no announcement himself. It was clear that Tenet was in the job at the sufferance of the White House and could be tossed at any moment.

Tenet quickly made the most of the opportunity. Bush decided to resume the daily intelligence briefings that Clinton had abandoned, and Tenet, at Bush's urging, attended them himself each day. That was a significant break from tradition; past CIA directors had allowed agency analysts to handle the briefings themselves. No other CIA director had ever scheduled himself to meet with the president every single morning to discuss the day's intelligence. By contrast, Clinton had completely abandoned his morning CIA briefing and simply read the written President's Daily Brief instead. But with Bush, Tenet went to the White House each morning, accompanied by a senior analyst who would provide the president with the regular daily briefing. Tenet would then talk with Bush personally about the most sensitive issues of the day.

Tenet prized his time with Bush, and it quickly paid off. After a morning intelligence briefing not long into the new administration, Bush told Tenet that he wanted him to stay. Let's keep this going, Bush told Tenet. It's working out. Tenet's closest and most loyal aides were soon bragging that Tenet had spent more time with Bush in just a few short months than he had spent with Clinton during his entire time in office.

Tenet kept his job despite some signs that the new national security advisor, Condoleezza Rice, was wary of him, just as some on the Clinton NSC staff had been before. Rice had a strong bullshit detector, and, according to former aides, that meant that she seemed on guard with Tenet. Some of Tenet's allies suspected, on the other hand, that Rice was jealous of Tenet's personal time with Bush; she wanted to be the ultimate gatekeeper. Much later in Bush's first term, their dislike became open and mutual. Tenet and many of his lieutenants came to believe that Rice was not an honest broker between the CIA and the president.

September 11 and its aftermath brought a unique dimension to the Bush-Tenet partnership. It was now forged in fire. After the attacks, Bush had to rely heavily on Tenet because he was the only person in the administration's inner circle who knew anything about Osama bin Laden and al Qaeda, particularly after White House counterterrorism czar Richard Clarke was shunted to the sidelines.

The U.S. military knew next to nothing about Afghanistan and was unprepared for war there. (The air force didn't even have updated maps of the country for its pilots, who in desperation turned to old Russian maps to help plot their missions.) By contrast, the CIA had a long history in Afghanistan, dating back to the covert action program in support of the Afghan rebels fighting the Soviet army in the 1980s. In the years just before 9/11, agency officers had also resumed intermittent contact with one of the old mujahideen leaders, Ahmed Masooud, the leader of the rebel Northern Alliance fighting the Taliban. Before 9/11, the CIA had talked, in vain, with Masooud about helping the Americans capture bin Laden. The CIA also had paid assets among certain tribes in southeastern Afghanistan who had been gathering intelligence about bin Laden's whereabouts. Bin Laden arranged to have Masooud murdered two days before the September 11 attacks, but the CIA still had enough contacts to lead the way into Afghanistan to battle al Qaeda and the Taliban that fall. Rumsfeld, the ultimate turf warrior, was deeply embarrassed that CIA officers were on the ground first, before the U.S. military, and that they were on hand to welcome Special Forces troops as they arrived in the country.

During those frantic days and weeks, Tenet was constantly at Bush's side. The tentative nature of their pre-9/11 relationship seemed long forgotten. In the weeks and months after September 11, Bush also came to Tenet's defense when questions about the CIA's performance before 9/11 began to emerge. Bush deflected critics of the CIA and refused to consider dismissing Tenet when the public began to wonder why no one was being held accountable for 9/11. "George and I have been spending a lot of quality time together," Bush told a crowd of CIA employees in late September 2001, the *Washington Times* reported the next day. "There's a reason. I've got a lot of confidence in him, and I've got a lot of confidence in the CIA."

In private that fall and winter, Tenet was extremely defensive about his agency's handling of terrorism and al Qaeda prior to 9/11. He denied that September 11 represented an intelligence failure. He had been CIA director since al Qaeda first became a major problem for the United States in the 1990s, and he seemed to view criticism on the issue as a personal attack. He and his aides insisted that they had provided adequate warning that al Qaeda was planning a major attack, and that that was as much as anyone could expect. Once the terrorists were inside the United States, Tenet and his aides liked to say, they had become an FBI problem. "We don't do America" was a line that began to come out of the seventh-floor executive suites at CIA headquarters. Tenet and his aides refused to accept the parallels between September 11 and Pearl Harbor, when the commander of the U.S. Navy's Pacific Fleet was relieved of command. They also grew increasingly angry as leading members of Congress began pushing for an investigation of the intelligence community's performance before September 11.

Tenet could never have maintained his defensive crouch if Bush had not provided him cover. Tenet was now in Bush's debt twice over: once for keeping him on after the election and again for protecting him after 9/11. By early 2002, Tenet's fortunes had become inextricably linked to those of Bush. That was also the period when the warmth of the Bush-Tenet relationship peaked. The sense of having shared a searing experience was still fresh and had not yet been dissipated by tensions over intelligence on Iraq. "George Tenet was too close to the president," one of Tenet's top lieutenants later acknowledged. "You shouldn't be the president's friend." At that moment, George Tenet was willing to do many things for George W. Bush.

In late March 2002, the National Security Agency obtained communications intercepts that indicated that Abu Zubaydah, a key lieutenant of Osama bin Laden, was hiding in Faisalabad, Pakistan, southwest of Lahore. Like most of al Qaeda's senior leadership, Zubaydah had fled Afghanistan as the Taliban government fell. He was now being harbored by local Islamic extremists. Some top al Qaeda leaders had made their way west to Iran after the ouster of the Taliban, but a large number, including Osama bin Laden, went south to Pakistan. Bin Laden and Ayman al-Zawahiri, his top deputy, found safe haven in the remote, mountainous tribal region along the Pakistani side of the Afghan-Pakistan border, but others, including Zubaydah, moved into Pakistan's urban areas, where they became easier targets for American intelligence.

The information on Zubaydah's location was precise enough to trigger late-night raids on several houses of suspected extremists in Faisalabad, conducted jointly by the CIA, FBI, and Pakistani security forces. The Pakistanis went into each house first, searching not just for Zubaydah but other operatives who might be hiding with him. In one house, a shootout erupted as the suspects made a run for it. One man was shot several times, including once in the groin, as he fled across the roof.

The Pakistanis handcuffed the wounded suspect and threw him into the back of a pickup truck along with several other captured militants. It was only when a senior FBI agent shined a light into the truck bed and recognized the face of the trussed and wounded man that anyone realized that Abu Zubaydah, the primary object of the raid, was bleeding to death. The terrorist was rushed to a Pakistani hospital. After his medical condition stabilized, he was secretly flown to Thailand and into CIA custody. The Thai government, which had long battled Muslim separatists in its southern provinces—and also had a history of cooperation with the U.S. military, dating back to Vietnam—was willing to be the first country to provide a secret location for the CIA to imprison and interrogate important al Qaeda prisoners.

Abu Zubaydah was the first high-ranking al Qaeda leader to fall into American hands after the September 11 attacks, and his capture was greeted with elation at the CIA and the White House. President Bush had famously called for Osama bin Laden's capture "dead or alive," and kept a CIA-generated list of top al Qaeda leaders so he could cross them off one by one as they were killed or captured. As it became increasingly clear that bin Laden had slipped through Bush's fingers, and that only one other major al Qaeda figure, Mohammed Atef, the terrorist network's chief of operations, had been killed in Afghanistan (in November 2001), Bush was painfully aware that most of al Qaeda's leadership still remained at large. Zubaydah's capture was a concrete and very welcome sign of progress in the Bush administration's new global war on terrorism.

There is a dispute about what happened next, largely because of the highly secretive nature of the Bush administration. According to a well-placed source with a proven track record of providing extremely reliable information to the author, George Tenet soon learned that George Bush was taking a very personal interest in the Zubaydah case.

Just days after Zubaydah's arrest, Tenet went to the White House to provide the president with his daily intelligence briefing and to discuss with him details of the Zubaydah case. According to the source, Bush asked Tenet what information the CIA was getting out of Zubaydah. Tenet responded that they weren't getting anything yet, because Abu Zubaydah had been so badly wounded that he was heavily medicated. He was too groggy from painkillers to talk coherently.

Bush turned to Tenet and asked: *"Who authorized putting him on pain medication?"*

It is possible that this was just one more piece of jocular banter between two plain-speaking men, according to the source who recounted this incident. Bush's phrasing was ambiguous.

But it is also possible that the comment meant something more. Was the president of the United States implicitly encouraging the director of Central Intelligence to order the harsh treatment of a prisoner? If so, this episode offers the most direct link yet between Bush and the harsh treatment of prisoners by both the CIA and the U.S. military. If Bush made the comment in order to push the CIA to get tough with Abu Zubaydah, he was doing so indirectly, without the paper trail that would have come from a written presidential authorization.

The occurrence of the exchange between Bush and Tenet has been challenged by some former senior Tenet lieutenants. While they say they can't deny that it ever happened, they say they have never heard of the incident and don't believe the story to be true.

Several former senior CIA officials also stress that Abu Zubaydah was given first-rate medical care that saved his life after he was discovered in the back of the Pakistani truck. There have been reports that pain medication was withheld from Abu Zubaydah after his medical condition stabilized. In his 2003 book, *Why America Slept,* author Gerald Posner reported that after Zubaydah had been stabilized he was administered a quick-acting narcotic infusion that would alternately be turned on to alleviate pain and turned off to make him feel pain.

Despite the dispute over the Tenet-Bush conversation concerning Abu Zubaydah and his pain medication, several current and former CIA officials say that after the September 11 attacks the president made it clear to agency officials in many ways that it was time for the gloves to come off. The reported Bush comment about pain medication for Abu Zubaydah fits into that broader, get-tough message that the president and the White House were sending to the CIA in the months after 9/11.

Two years after Abu Zubaydah's capture, the Iraqi prisoner abuse scandal erupted, triggered by photographs of degrading and pornographic treatment of detainees at Abu Ghraib prison and expanded with further disclosures of abuse by the U.S. military and the CIA. No one has ever been able to link George W. Bush directly to the chain of events that led to the prisoner abuse. The White House steadfastly maintained that President Bush was horrified by the images of torture and that he had never personally approved the harsh interrogation methods employed against Iraqis, Afghans, and other prisoners. According to the White House's version of events, Bush remained far above the dark side of the war on terror.

In the many news stories about the abuse scandal, including those that described administration deliberations about the legal basis for harsh interrogation tactics, Bush was an absent figure. It was as if the interrogation policies were developed in a presidential vacuum. When legal opinions written by Justice Department lawyers approving harsh tactics were made public, the reaction of the White House was to downplay their significance and argue that the president had always insisted that prisoners be treated humanely.

The Abu Ghraib scandal eventually ebbed, in part because of the lack of proof that the president had ordered the mistreatment of prisoners. In June 2004, just after the Abu Ghraib photos first emerged, Bush insisted that he would never order torture. "Let me make very clear the position of my government and our country," he told reporters. "We do not condone torture. I have never ordered torture. I will never order torture. The values of this country are such that torture is not a part of our soul and our being." He added that "the United States will continue to take seriously the need to question terrorists who have information that can save lives. But we will not compromise the rule of law or the values and principles that make us strong. Torture is wrong no matter where it occurs, and the United States will continue to lead the fight to eliminate it everywhere."

There is evidence that senior administration officials, apparently including Vice President Dick Cheney, made certain to protect the president from personal involvement in the internal debates on the handling of prisoners. The CIA's Office of Inspector General, which has been investigating evidence of the agency's involvement in prisoner abuse, has found that there was never any written form of presidential authorization covering the CIA's interrogation tactics used on detainees in its custody, according to a CIA official familiar with the IG investigation. The president was never officially briefed on the tactics being used, the IG found. George Tenet gave briefings on the CIA's interrogation tactics to Vice President Cheney and a very small group of other top officials, including National Security Advisor Condoleezza Rice, Attorney General John Ashcroft, and then White House counsel Alberto Gonzalez, according to a CIA official.

Normally, such high-stakes—and very secret—CIA activities would be carefully vetted by the White House and legally authorized in writing by the president under what are known as presidential findings. Such directives are required by Congress when the CIA engages in covert action. In the days after 9/11, President Bush signed a covert action finding authorizing the CIA to kill or capture and detain al Qaeda operatives around the world, but the finding was silent on the interrogation tactics to be used on those in detention.

Officials say that Tenet never demanded written presidential authorization for the interrogation techniques, and he agreed not to go into the Oval Office and describe in detail in a formal presidential briefing what the CIA was doing with captured al Qaeda operatives and other prisoners. It is not clear whether Tenet was told by Cheney or other senior White House officials not to brief Bush or whether he made that decision on his own. It is also possible that Bush made it clear to Tenet what he wanted done, and that Tenet decided not to ask for written orders.

Certainly, Cheney and senior White House officials knew that Bush was purposely not being briefed and that the CIA was not being given written presidential authorization for its tactics. It appears that there was a secret agreement among very senior administration officials to insulate Bush and to give him deniability, even as his vice president and senior lieutenants were meeting to discuss the harsh new interrogation methods. President Bush was following a "don't ask, don't tell" policy on the treatment of prisoners.

When reporters asked the White House whether President Bush had approved of torture or harsh interrogation practices, they were asking the wrong question. The right question was whether George W. Bush had been given plausible deniability by his own inner circle.

The failure to demand explicit and written presidential approval for the interrogation practices may come back to haunt the CIA in the future. "I think [senior CIA officials] wanted to be more Catholic than the Pope, so they went ahead and just did it, and did it without explicit presidential authorization," said a CIA source familiar with the CIA Inspector General's investigation of prisoner abuse. "There was no explicit presidential approval."

The most significant written approval obtained by the CIA for its interrogation practices came from a Justice Department legal opinion authorizing the use of harsh tactics. That classified legal opinion was requested specifically for the case of Abu Zubaydah. The agency wanted to provide some legal protections for officers involved in the Zubaydah interrogations. (In fact, a key difference between the instances of prisoner abuse committed by the U.S. military at Abu Ghraib and the harsh tactics used by the CIA is that the CIA's practices at least had some explicit and written high-level authorization.) In that opinion, the Justice Department's lawyers determined that the harsh tactics were allowed under the doctrine of self-defense. Abu Zubaydah might have information about future terrorist attacks against the United States, and so the CIA was justified in playing rough in an effort to obtain information that could save American lives. CIA officials believe that Justice Department opinion gave them sufficient legal protection for their actions. Still, some agency officials later expressed concern and frustration that Tenet had not demanded and obtained written presidential authorization in order to make clear in the future what they believed to be true— that they were doing what George W. Bush wanted them to do. According to a CIA source, one senior CIA official interviewed by the CIA Inspector General told the IG staff that he regretted the fact that Tenet and other senior agency officials had not gone into the Oval Office and looked the president in the eye and specifically briefed him on their interrogation methods.

In order to avoid a requirement for a presidential finding, the CIA determined that the interrogation tactics should be considered a part of the agency's normal "intelligence collection," rather than be defined as covert action. That semantic difference allowed the CIA to conduct the interrogations without specific presidential approval. "This was not considered a covert action, and so there was no finding, no MON [a CIA acronym for memorandum of notification, the procedure by which covert action findings are amended to provide approval for specific operations]," said a CIA source. "It was considered part of intelligence collection."

In many ways, the Abu Zubaydah case was the critical precedent for the future handling of prisoners both in the global war on terrorism and in the war in Iraq. The harsh interrogation methods the CIA used on Zubaydah prompted the first wide-ranging legal and policy review establishing the procedures to be followed in the detention of future detainees. "Abu Zubaydah's capture triggered everything," explained a CIA source. In the process, the CIA became the principal interrogators of high-value detainees—and the first U.S. agency to develop controversial interrogation techniques.

The Bush administration's authorization of those techniques, for first use by the CIA on Abu Zubaydah, created a permissive climate that eventually permeated the entire government and transformed American attitudes toward the handling of prisoners. Once the CIA, which had no history of running prisons or of handling large numbers of prisoners, was given the green light to use harsh methods, the United States military, which had a proud tradition of adhering to the Geneva Conventions, began to get signals from the Bush administration that the rules had changed.

Prior to Zubaydah's arrest, the United States had mostly captured low-level fighters off the battlefields of Afghanistan, and only a few had significant intelligence value. At first, the United States and its Afghan allies held Taliban and foreign Arab fighters—defined by the Bush administration as enemy combatants rather than prisoners of war—in medieval conditions in overcrowded Afghan prisons. It quickly became obvious that a longer-term solution was needed both to deal with the rising numbers of prisoners and in order to interrogate them in isolation.

In response, in January 2002, after considering several alternative sites, the U.S. military established a prison camp at the U.S. Navy base at Guantánamo Bay, Cuba, and began airlifting prisoners from Afghanistan into the new prison, named Camp X-Ray. The first prisoners arrived on January 11, 2002.

While the U.S. military was flying Afghan grunts to Guantánamo, President Bush chose the CIA, over the FBI and the Pentagon, to take the lead in handling senior al Qaeda prisoners. By choosing the CIA over the FBI, Bush was rejecting the law enforcement approach to fighting terrorism that had been favored during the Clinton era. Bush had decided that al Qaeda was a national security threat, not a law enforcement problem, and he did not want al Qaeda operatives brought back to face trial in the United States, where they would come under the strict rules of the American legal system. That meant the FBI, which had taken the lead in criminal investigations of al Qaeda prior to 9/11, would be pushed to the sidelines.

For FBI agents in the field in Afghanistan, the first sign that they had lost the turf battle for control of al Qaeda prisoners to the CIA came in late 2001, in the case of Ibn al-Shaykh al-Libi, who had run an al Qaeda training camp in Afghanistan until his November 2001 capture. At first, al-Libi, one of the first al Qaeda operatives captured in the Afghan war, was questioned by the FBI at Baghram Air Base outside Kabul. When the FBI agents began to coax al-Libi's cooperation, they advised him of his Miranda rights. The FBI agents believed he would be flown back to the United States for prosecution. In those early weeks after 9/11, the FBI was still thinking first about criminal prosecutions of al Qaeda operatives—not torturing them in secret overseas prisons.

The FBI believed that al-Libi could be useful as a witness against Zacharias Moussaoui, the French-Moroccan flight student who had been picked up on immigration charges in Minnesota just before 9/11 and who was the only person in the United States facing prosecution in connection with those attacks. "Hanging over this was Moussaoui," recalled an FBI source involved in the al-Libi case. "What do we have against Moussaoui? We were thinking that we could get this guy to testify against Moussaoui."

The CIA, however, had no interest in allowing al-Libi to set foot in the United States. In the end, CIA officers simply came and took al-Libi away from the FBI in Afghanistan, according to the FBI source. The agency flew him to Egypt, where Egyptian intelligence, an organization known to have tortured prisoners, interrogated him on behalf of the agency. According to the FBI source, as the CIA took the prisoners away, an FBI agent overheard one CIA officer say to al-Libi: *You know where you are going. Before you get there, I am going to find your mother and fuck her.*

By this point, George Tenet and the CIA were rapidly gaining in power and turf. Before long, the CIA would have its own prison system. With a mandate to take charge of top al Qaeda detainees, the CIA quickly vetoed Camp X-Ray at Guantánamo as a place to hold important prisoners. CIA officers reported back to Langley from Guantánamo that there were too many American officials, from too many different agencies, all conducting interrogations and all trying to get in on a piece of the action, and all trying to prove that they could be the first to obtain a nugget of intelligence from the sorry lot of Afghans and Arabs being held there. Long before there were concerns within the CIA or elsewhere in the government about prisoner abuse at Guantánamo, there was a widely shared view within the CIA that Camp X-Ray had turned chaotic, a "goat fuck."

Worse, it was too public. The CIA wanted secret locations where it could have complete control over the interrogations and debrief-ings, free from the prying eyes of the international media, free from monitoring by human rights groups, and, most important, far from the jurisdiction of the American legal system. The CIA assigned a group of agency officials to try to find alternative prison sites in coun-tries scattered around the world. They were studying, said one CIA source, "how to make people disappear."

There were a number of third world countries, with dubious human rights records, willing to play host. One African country offered the CIA the use of an island in the middle of a large lake, ac-cording to CIA sources, and other nations were equally accommo-dating. Eventually, several CIA prisons were secretly established, including at least two major ones, code-named Bright Light and Salt Pit. A small group of officials within the CIA's Counterterrorist Center was put in charge of supporting the prisons and managing the interrogations.

CIA sources say that Salt Pit is in Afghanistan and is used to house low-level prisoners. Bright Light is one of the prisons where top al Qaeda leaders—including Abu Zubaydah and Khalid Sheikh Mohammed, the central planner of the September 11 attacks—have been held. Bright Light's location is secret, and it has been used for only a handful of the most important al Qaeda detainees. CIA sources say that the agency has repeatedly moved the most important detainees from one hidden prison to another in order to keep their lo-cations secret. In addition to Thailand, the CIA has established secret prisons in Eastern Europe, reportedly in Poland and Romania. But the CIA is believed to have secret prisons in other locations around the world as well. (Eventually, the CIA set up one of its secret prisons in Guantánamo, separate from the main Camp X-Ray, but closed it down after U.S. court rulings began to cast doubt on whether prison-ers held in Guantánamo would come under the protection of U.S. law. Later, the U.S. military built new, more permanent prison facil-ities at Guantánamo to replace Camp X-Ray.)

The exact locations and nature of the CIA prisons housing high-value al Qaeda detainees are still among the most closely guarded secrets in the government. Within the CIA's Counterterrorist Center, the locations of the prisons for high-value detainees are so secret that analysts are not allowed to send questions to be asked of the prisoners directly to the prisons. Instead, according to one former CTC official, CTC analysts must turn over their questions to the small group within CTC managing the prisons. That group then sends the questions to interrogators. "That was the way they tried to make sure you never knew anything about the prisons," said one CTC veteran.

CIA officers soon learned one thing for sure—prisoners sent to Bright Light and the other facilities handling high-value detainees were probably never going to be released. "The word is that once you get sent to Bright Light, you never come back," said the CTC veteran.

To be sure, the Bush administration has not yet decided what to do with top al Qaeda operatives after they have been drained of all intelligence value. Several senior CIA officials have expressed eagerness to get out of the prison business, but they are not yet sure how they can extricate themselves from it.

Meanwhile, as the CIA's network of prisons grew, many CIA officers began to shudder at what was happening to their agency. A poisonous new culture was taking root. The CIA was building a dark infrastructure that no one wanted to talk about. For many CIA case officers, this was not the job they had signed up for when they enlisted in American espionage.

"I kept wondering, how did we get into the prison business?" said one source who worked in the CTC. "Why was the CIA doing this? This wasn't what we had been trained for."

The CIA's interrogation techniques were based on methods used in the training of U.S. Special Forces soldiers to prepare them for the possibility of being captured. The tactics were designed to simulate torture, but they are supposed to stop short of inflicting serious injury. Among the most controversial techniques approved for use on high-ranking al Qaeda detainees by CIA interrogators was something known as water boarding, in which a prisoner was strapped down and made to believe he might drown.

The assertions that the CIA's tactics stopped short of torture were undercut by the fact that the FBI decided that the tactics were so severe that the bureau wanted no part of them, and FBI agents were ordered to stay away from the CIA-run interrogations. FBI agents did briefly see Abu Zubaydah in custody, and at least one agent came away convinced that Zubaydah was being tortured, according to an FBI source.

Several CIA officials who are familiar with the way the interrogations of high-value al Qaeda detainees are actually conducted say that there are no doubts in their minds that the CIA is torturing its prisoners. Water boarding is used, not just once to simulate torture, but over and over again, according to one CIA source. According to several intelligence sources, a secret CIA report describes how Khalid Sheikh Mohammed was subjected to the application of several types of harsh interrogation techniques approximately a hundred times over a period of two weeks. Prisoners have been forced into coffin-like boxes, forced into cells where they are alternately denied all light and put in brightly lit rooms and denied sleep for long periods. They are subjected to long hours of extremely loud rap music—Eminem is one favorite—and they are forced to stand or squat in "stress positions" for hours at a time. "If you read the interrogation reports, you see that what is being done is torture," said a CIA source who has read some of the reports. "It is the accumulation of all of the procedures, and how frequently they are being used, that makes it torture. The reports are horrifying to read." The CIA has refused to grant any independent observer or human rights group access to the high-level detainees to determine their physical and mental health.

Supporters of the use of harsh or even abusive interrogation techniques have argued that they are necessary in a new and unconventional war against suicidal terrorists who don't abide by the traditional rules of war themselves. But many CIA officers and other critics of the interrogation tactics have warned that they are not effective, because prisoners will say anything that they think their interrogators want to hear in order to get them to stop the abuse. Torture generates bad information.

Such warnings have now proven accurate. According to a well-placed CIA source, Khalid Sheikh Mohammed, the central planner of the 9/11 plot and the most important al Qaeda prisoner in U.S. custody, has now recanted some of what he previously told the CIA during his interrogations. That is an enormous setback for the CIA, since debriefings of Khalid Sheikh Mohammed had been considered among the agency's most important sources of intelligence on al Qaeda. It is unclear precisely which of his earlier statements Khalid Sheikh Mohammed has now disavowed, but any recantation by the most important prisoner in the global war on terror must call into question much of what the United States has obtained from other prisoners around the world, including those from Iraq.

The CIA abuse scandal goes to the heart of George Tenet's post-9/11 CIA. In many ways, Tenet was a transitional figure, a CIA director who had the adroit political skills to straddle the pre- and post-9/11 worlds, and who had adapted his management of the U.S. intelligence community to both. But that straddle left him open to two kinds of criticism. Before 9/11, George Tenet's CIA faced criticism, including from many of the agency's own officers, for being paralyzed by political correctness and risk aversion. After 9/11, George

Tenet's CIA began to conduct secret activities that deeply concerned some of the agency's own officers.

Related to torture, one of the most troubling practices of Tenet's new CIA was the aggressive use of "renditions"—the practice of secretly transporting prisoners to other countries for interrogation, sometimes to Arab countries such as Egypt and Syria that are known to practice torture. The CIA conducted renditions for several years before 9/11, but the use of renditions—and the kind of renditions conducted—changed radically after the September 11 attacks. The CIA and the Bush administration have repeatedly stated that they do not send prisoners to other countries to be tortured and that they received assurances from the governments of those countries that the prisoners will not be abused. But since 9/11, the practice has become so widespread, and enough people caught up in renditions have been released and gone public with their experiences, that the facts seem to belie the CIA's claims.

While several rendition cases that involved innocent people or have otherwise gone badly have been documented in the press, many of the worst aspects of the CIA's rendition operations have remained hidden.

One CIA officer haunted by what he saw in one particular rendition described the case to the author. This officer alleged that the CIA flew a prisoner from Afghanistan to a country in the Persian Gulf—where he was to be turned over to local authorities and imprisoned again—despite knowing that he was an innocent man who had been wrongly identified as a terrorist. The CIA officer said he believed that the CIA was moving the prisoner in order to hide its mistake. The officer said that when the prisoner arrived in the Persian Gulf country, the local security service fingerprinted the man and determined that he was not the suspect that the CIA had claimed it was turning over. The local security service refused to take the man into custody, and the CIA flew him back to Afghanistan. The CIA officer said he later found out that the man, who was from an African country, was a refugee who had purchased a passport on the open market for $50; the passport was in the name of a terrorist suspect.

The man had been held by the CIA for months in Afghanistan without anyone at the agency correcting the mistake. The CIA officer also later was told that the CIA station chief in the prisoner's native country in Africa had sent cables to CIA headquarters stating that the agency was holding the wrong man. The CIA officer said he did not know what happened to the man after he was flown back to Afghanistan. Other CIA officials say that the account provided to the author sounds similar to a case that has been under investigation by the CIA's office of the Inspector General.

In the intense atmosphere after the September 11 attacks, even more radical and questionable operations were considered and planned. One such secret activity was code-named Box Top. In 2002, according to CIA sources, the agency created a covert paramilitary unit whose mission was to go around the world to target terrorists. Whether the Box Top unit would have had the mandate to kill terrorists anywhere in the world or simply to capture them and bring them back through the rendition process is unclear. But after the unit was set up and began training, it was disbanded, and Box Top never went into effect. CIA sources suggested that the agency's top management got cold feet over the prospect of turning the paramilitary unit loose.

Today it is still difficult to obtain accurate figures on how many people are imprisoned around the world by the U.S. military and the CIA. The CIA is believed to be holding about a hundred prisoners, including two or three dozen high-value detainees, but the agency won't confirm the identities of the prisoners in its custody. Another obstacle to tracking the CIA's prison population has been the agency's willingness to hide prisoners, keeping them off the books. Such "ghost detainees" sparked controversy when the practice was disclosed in Iraq.

There has so far been relatively little accountability within the CIA for the allegations of abuse of prisoners in its custody. There have been isolated cases of reprimands and punishment. CIA officials have confirmed, for example, that one CIA employee was disciplined for threatening an al Qaeda prisoner with a gun during questioning, while separately, a contract employee was charged with beating a prisoner to death in Afghanistan. But there is no evidence that any top CIA officials have been disciplined or faced serious investigations into their actions. In that respect, the CIA is much like the U.S. military, where investigations into cases of prisoner abuse have focused primarily on low-level enlisted personnel rather than senior officers or top Defense Department policy makers.

But a difficult legal problem for the agency could still emerge as a result of the agency's involvement in the secret renditions of prisoners out of Iraq, according to a CIA source. The CIA took the prisoners out of Iraq to be detained and interrogated in other countries. According to the CIA source, that practice appears to be in direct violation of the Geneva Conventions and could be defined as a "grave breach" under international law. Under a 1996 U.S. law, a "grave breach" of the Geneva Conventions constitutes a war crime in the United States, and so is a crime under federal law. The CIA's Inspector General has issued a criminal referral to the Justice Department on the matter, according to the CIA source.

The establishment of a series of secret prisons around the world and the widespread use of harsh interrogation tactics against prisoners in American custody has been part of a broader and disquieting pattern by the Bush administration. The White House has interpreted the constitutional powers of the president to fight terrorism in such an expansive way that long-standing rules governing the military and intelligence communities have been skirted or ignored, and secret intelligence activities inside the United States have been approved that may be violating the civil liberties of American citizens.

In particular, the technical wizards of the National Security Agency have been engaged in a program of domestic data mining that is so vast, and so unprecedented, that it makes a mockery of long-standing privacy rules.

2

THE PROGRAM

I N FEBRUARY 1999, Michael Hayden, a balding and soft-spoken air force lieutenant general from Pennsylvania, was nominated by President Bill Clinton to become the director of the National Security Agency, the largest organization in the United States intelligence community, double the size of the CIA and truly the dominant electronic spy service in the world. For Hayden, a military intelligence officer who had begun his career as an analyst at the Strategic Air Command at the height of the Cold War, the new assignment was the great reward for nearly thirty years of hard slogging up the chain of command, for persistence in a career that Hayden must have at some point considered a dead end, particularly after a four-year assignment in the 1970s in the most obscure corner of the air force, as an ROTC instructor at tiny St. Michael's College in Winooski, Vermont.

Hayden was stationed in South Korea, serving in a senior staff position, when this big promotion came. Coincidentally, Hollywood had just released a movie about the NSA, and it was showing in Korea as Hayden was preparing for his new assignment. Mike Hayden couldn't resist going to see Will Smith and Gene Hackman in *Enemy of the State*.

Hayden was appalled. The movie showed the NSA as an evil, rogue organization that used its cutting-edge technology to spy on and persecute unwitting Americans. After thoroughly penetrating every aspect of his life, an NSA team of assassins tries to kill Will Smith, who plays a Washington lawyer whom the NSA bosses suspect knows too much about the agency's dark side. Smith is saved only after he befriends Gene Hackman, playing a reclusive former NSA technical wizard who turns the tables on the agency and helps Smith get the truth out.

The film's message—that the NSA is an uncontrollable beast run by a cadre of ruthless bureaucrats secretly trampling on the civil rights of Americans—sent shivers through Hayden. *Enemy of the State* was one of the most prominent movies ever made about the NSA, and it reinforced every dark nightmare the American public had about the government's supersecret eavesdropping and code-breaking apparatus.

The movie came out just as a controversy over the NSA was breaking out in Europe as well, thanks to the agency's global surveillance programs, known publicly as Echelon, through which it vacuums up communications around the world outside the United States. European politicians (outside of the United Kingdom, where the Government Communications Headquarters, GCHQ, Britain's version of the NSA, cooperates with U.S. eavesdropping operations) were bitter that the United States was targeting its giant eavesdropping machinery at them, and their anger prompted some Americans to wonder whether Echelon was ever turned on inside the United States for use against political dissidents. The Electronic Privacy Information Center, a Washington group that tries to keep up with NSA activities, went to court to try to discover whether Echelon or similar programs were being used to spy on Americans.

For an intelligence bureaucrat, Hayden responded to the controversies over *Enemy of the State* and Echelon in an unorthodox and creative way. Instead of denying the film's cultural influence, or the growing public uneasiness over NSA's power, he realized that his agency had to open itself up to greater scrutiny in order to disprove the conspiracy theorists. The NSA, whose very existence had once been a state secret, had to start talking about itself, and it had to start dealing with the press.

This was unprecedented for the NSA, and it was disorienting and shocking for the agency's old hands, who had been trained never, ever, to discuss their jobs, even with their husbands or wives. The NSA was, at heart, a blue-collar spy agency. It operated the intelligence plumbing, and so it tended to attract quiet technicians, math and linguistics geeks, and military and civilian managers who were bureaucratic conformists. None of them understood Hayden's desire to deal with the outside world, let alone the press. They knew that the public image of the NSA was a badly distorted cartoon, and they also knew that the agency had actually accomplished remarkable—and politically risky—things on behalf of the United States, almost none of which had ever become public.

For example, in 1990 the CIA and NSA jointly stole virtually every code machine (and their manuals) in use by the Soviet Union, giving NSA's code breakers a remarkable advantage on Moscow. The CIA and NSA obtained the Soviet code machines in Prague and then flew them to NSA headquarters at Fort Meade, Maryland, to be carefully dissected. The operation was an espionage triumph, but one that NSA officials would never consider discussing publicly, even many years later. Better to let public misunderstandings about NSA fester, the old-timers believed, than to disclose the agency's successes.

But if NSA didn't start talking, Hayden feared, then urban legends about the agency would take hold in the national imagination, and support for it and its mission would erode. "I made the judgment that we couldn't survive with the popular impression of this agency being formed by the last Will Smith movie," Hayden told CNN. The agency, Hayden promised, had learned its lesson from the dark days of the 1970s, when the domestic abuses of the FBI, the CIA—and the NSA—were revealed by congressional committees chaired by Idaho senator Frank Church and New York congressman Otis Pike. Church and Pike discovered that the NSA had been involved, along with the FBI, in domestic spying on activists in the civil rights and anti–Vietnam War movements.

The NSA had been created in 1952 by President Harry Truman in order to consolidate the government's code-breaking and code-making capabilities, and initially there were few legal limits on the NSA's ability to conduct electronic surveillance inside the United States. But in the wake of the Church and Pike committee disclosures, Congress passed a law in 1978 that required search warrants, approved by a secret court, for domestic wiretaps in national security cases. That law, the Foreign Intelligence Surveillance Act (FISA), along with other new rules and regulations imposed on the intelligence community in the 1970s and 1980s, effectively ended the NSA's role in domestic surveillance operations.

After those rules were put in place, the FBI, not the NSA, became the primary agency responsible for seeking approval from a special FISA court for national security wiretaps inside the United States. The NSA's domestic role was limited largely to such specialized intelligence activities as the bugging of foreign embassies and diplomatic missions in Washington, New York, and other cities, but even those operations required FISA search warrants.

Hayden wanted the American people to know that the NSA was abiding by the rules.

"Could there be abuses? Of course, there could, but I am looking you and the American people in the eye and saying there are not," Hayden told CNN. "After Church and Pike, on this question, the ball and strike count on the agency is no balls and two strikes," Hayden added. "We don't take any pitches that are close to the strike zone. We are very, very careful. We can't go back to the American people with, 'Oh, well, we're sorry for this one, too.' We don't get close to the Fourth Amendment."

Hayden gave speeches. He went on television, and he talked to newspaper reporters and to authors writing books about the agency. He even hosted off-the-record dinners for the press at his home at Fort Meade. A key element of Hayden's case was his argument that the NSA was struggling to cope with the rapid pace of change in an age of information overload, a new world of cell phones and Black-Berries and Internet telephone calls. The NSA was collecting more communications than anyone could ever listen to; even its supercomputers, with artificial-intelligence software, had trouble sorting the wheat from the chaff. Downplaying the NSA's capabilities, Hayden liked to say that the NSA was once an information-age organization in the industrial age, and now it was an information-age organization in the information age. It was losing its competitive edge. Commercially available communications technology was catching up. Hayden's implicit message was that the NSA was too archaic, maybe even too incompetent, to spy on America. Hayden didn't say that the NSA was a toothless giant, but he certainly wanted everyone to believe that the NSA was not to be feared.

"Despite what you've seen on television, our agency doesn't do alien autopsies, track the location of your automobile by satellite, nor do we have a squad of assassins," Hayden said reassuringly in a speech at American University in Washington in 2000. "The best I can hope for now is to wipe away some of the mystique surrounding the National Security Agency."

But that was Michael Hayden before 9/11.

Since the attacks, the NSA, with Hayden at the helm until 2005, has been transformed by the Bush administration, in ways that Hayden and other administration officials don't want to talk about. In fact, for the first time since the Watergate-era abuses, the NSA is spying on Americans again, and on a large scale.

The Bush administration has swept aside nearly thirty years of rules and regulations and has secretly brought the NSA back into the business of domestic espionage. The NSA is now eavesdropping on as many as five hundred people in the United States at any given time and it potentially has access to the phone calls and e-mails of millions more. It does this without court-approved search warrants and with little independent oversight.

President Bush has secretly authorized the NSA to monitor and eavesdrop on large volumes of telephone calls, e-mail messages, and other Internet traffic inside the United States to search for potential evidence of terrorist activity, without search warrants or any new laws that would permit such domestic intelligence collection. Under a secret presidential order signed in early 2002, only months after the September 11 attacks, President Bush has given the NSA the ability to conduct surveillance on communications inside the United States. The secret decision by the president has opened up America's domestic telecommunications network to the NSA in unprecedented and deeply troubling new ways, and represents a radical shift in the accepted policies and practices of the modern U.S. intelligence community.

The NSA is now tapping into the heart of the nation's telephone network through direct access to key telecommunications switches that carry many of America's daily phone calls and e-mail messages. Several government officials who know about the NSA operation have come forward to talk about it because they are deeply troubled by it, and they believe that by keeping silent they would become complicit in it. They strongly believe that the president's secret order is in violation of the Fourth Amendment of the Constitution, which prohibits unreasonable searches, and some of them believe that an investigation should be launched into the way the Bush administration has turned the intelligence community's most powerful tools against the American people.

One government lawyer who is aware of the NSA domestic surveillance operation told reporter Eric Lichtblau that the very few people at the Justice Department who are aware of its existence simply refer to it as "the Program." It may be the largest domestic spying operation since the 1960s, larger than anything conducted by the FBI or CIA inside the United States since the Vietnam War.

In order to overturn the system established by FISA in 1978, and bring the NSA back into domestic wiretaps without court approval, administration lawyers have issued a series of secret legal opinions, similar to those written in support of the harsh interrogation tactics used on detainees captured in Iraq and Afghanistan. The Bush administration legal opinions that supported the use of harsh interrogation techniques on al Qaeda detainees have, of course, proven controversial, drawing complaints from allies, objections from civil liberties advocates, and court challenges. The administration faced its first serious legal rebuke in June 2004 when the U.S. Supreme Court rejected the administration's effort to hold "enemy combatants" without a hearing. The court warned that "a state of war is not a blank check for the president."

The same could be said about the Program. Yet the NSA domestic spying operation has remained secret, and so the legal opinions and other documents related to the NSA program are still classified.

The administration apparently has several legal opinions to support the NSA operation, written by lawyers at the White House, the CIA, the NSA, and the Justice Department. They all rely heavily on a broad interpretation of Article Two of the Constitution, which grants power to the president as commander in chief of the armed forces. Relying largely on those constitutional powers, Congress passed a resolution just days after the September 11 attacks granting the president the authority to wage a global war on terrorism, and Bush administration lawyers later decided that the war resolution provided the legal basis they needed to support the NSA operation to eavesdrop on American citizens.

While the Bush administration has never publicly discussed the NSA operation, the Justice Department did hint at the administration's thinking on domestic spying in a little-noticed legal brief in an unrelated court case in 2002. That brief said that "the Constitution vests in the president inherent authority to conduct warrantless intelligence surveillance (electronic or otherwise) of foreign powers or their agents, and Congress cannot by statute extinguish that constitutional authority." The search for foreign "agents" has led the NSA to peer into domestic streams of data.

Debate within the government about the moral and legal issues involved in the NSA operation has been extremely limited because only a handful of high-ranking government officials are aware of the existence of the eavesdropping program. "It was a closed program," said one very senior administration official. "People normally in the chain didn't have access to it."

At the Justice Department, then–Attorney General John Ashcroft was one of the few people informed, and he then brought in a small, select group of like-minded conservative lawyers to help craft some of the legal opinions to buttress the Program. They may have been some of the same lawyers involved in the legal opinions supporting the harsh interrogation techniques.

The NSA eavesdropping operation has been hidden inside a "special access program," a level of secrecy reserved for the government's most sensitive covert operations. "This is the biggest secret I know about," said one official who was deeply troubled by what he knew.

Bush administration officials justify the presidential order by arguing that existing rules curbing the domestic powers of the NSA and CIA impeded the United States in detecting and preventing terrorist attacks. They say that the NSA domestic spying operation is critical to the global war on terrorism, although they offer few specifics. They have not explained why any terrorist would be so naïve as to assume that his electronic communication was impossible to intercept.

* * *

The small handful of experts on national security law within the government who know about the NSA program say they believe it has made a mockery of the public debate over the Patriot Act. The Patriot Act of 2001 has been widely criticized for giving the government too much power to engage in secret searches and to spy on suspects, and even some Republicans chafed at the idea of giving the government still more surveillance powers under an extended and expanded version. The Patriot Act has increased the ability of the nation's intelligence and law-enforcement agencies to monitor conversations and Internet traffic by terrorist suspects with the approval of the special FISA court. But it still requires the FBI to obtain search warrants from the FISA court each time it wants to eavesdrop on a telephone conversation, e-mail message, or other form of communication within the United States. In order to obtain a warrant from the FISA court, the FBI must present evidence to show that the target is linked to a terrorist organization or other foreign agent or power. Even then, the FBI has, in comparison with the NSA, relatively limited technological resources and doesn't have the ability to monitor huge telecommunications networks. It lacks NSA's banks of supercomputers at Fort Meade, believed to be home to the greatest concentration of computing power in the world.

The Patriot Act has given no new powers to the NSA. The Bush administration purposely did not seek congressional approval for the NSA operation, apparently because the White House recognized that it would be too controversial and would almost certainly be rejected. "There is nothing explicit in the Patriot Act for NSA," said one former congressional aide who was involved in the drafting of the Patriot Act, but who was unaware of the NSA operation. "Their surveillance is supposed to be directed outside the United States."

It is now clear that the White House went through the motions of the public debate over the Patriot Act, all the while knowing that the intelligence community was secretly conducting a far more aggressive domestic surveillance campaign. "This goes way beyond the Patriot Act," said one former official familiar with the NSA operation.

President Bush's secret order has given the NSA the freedom to employ extremely powerful computerized search programs—originally intended to scan foreign communications—in order to scrutinize large volumes of American communications. It is difficult to know the precise size of the NSA operation, but one indication of its large scale is the fact that administration officials say that one reason they decided not to seek court-approved search warrants for the NSA operation was that the volume of telephone calls and e-mails being monitored was so big that it would be impossible to get speedy court approval for all of them. It is certainly true that when the FISA court was created, Congress never envisioned that the NSA would be involved in a massive eavesdropping operation inside the United States. No one in the 1970s could have predicted the enormous growth of telecommunications traffic in the United States, or the degree to which Americans would become addicted to digital, electronic communications. Today, industry experts estimate that approximately 9 trillion e-mails are sent in the United States each year. Americans make nearly a billion cell phone calls and well over a billion landline calls each day.

NSA's technical prowess, coupled with its long-standing relationships with the nation's major telecommunications companies, has made it easy for the agency to eavesdrop on large numbers of people in the United States without their knowledge. Following President Bush's order, U.S. intelligence officials secretly arranged with top officials of major telecommunications companies to gain access to large telecommunications switches carrying the bulk of America's phone calls. The NSA also gained access to the vast majority of American e-mail traffic that flows through the U.S. telecommunications system. The identities of the companies involved have been kept secret. Unknown to most Americans, the NSA has extremely close relationships with both the telecommunications and computer industries, according to several government officials. Only a very few top executives in each corporation are aware of such relationships or know about the willingness of the corporations to cooperate on intelligence matters.

The main rationale behind the Program, officials said, was that existing rules curbing the domestic powers of the NSA and CIA had left gaps in the ability of the United States to detect and prevent terrorist attacks. They say that one such gap had opened up because many purely international communications—telephone calls and e-mail messages from the Middle East to Asia, for example—end up going through telecommunications switches that are physically based in the United States. As a result, the rules that limit domestic intelligence gathering by the NSA have meant that such international calls could not be monitored, since they were transiting the United States. Some phone calls and e-mail traffic among terrorists operating overseas were being missed by American counterterrorism investigators.

The new presidential order has given the NSA direct access to those U.S.-based telecommunications switches through "back doors." Under the authority of the presidential order, a small group of officials at NSA now monitors telecommunications activity through these domestic switches, searching for terrorism-related intelligence.

To understand how the Bush administration is spying on the American people, it is important to know a few basics about the U.S. telecommunications network. The telephone network today is digital and computerized, but is still built around a switching system that routes calls from city to city, or country to country, as efficiently and quickly as possible.

In addition to handling telephone calls from, say, Los Angeles to New York, the switches also act as gateways into and out of the United States for international telecommunications. A large volume of purely international telephone calls—calls that do not begin or end in America—also now travel through switches based in the United States. Telephone calls from Asia to Europe, for example, may go through the United States–based switches. This so-called transit traffic has dramatically increased in recent years as the telephone network has become increasingly globalized. Computerized systems determine the most efficient routes for digital "packets" of electronic communications depending on the speed and congestion on the networks, not necessarily on the shortest line between two points. Such random global route selection means that the switches carrying calls from Cleveland to Chicago, for example, may also be carrying calls from Islamabad to Jakarta. In fact, it is now difficult to tell where the domestic telephone system ends and the international network begins.

In the years before 9/11, the NSA apparently recognized that the remarkable growth in transit traffic was becoming a major issue that had never been addressed by FISA or the other 1970s-era rules and regulations governing the U.S. intelligence community. Now that foreign calls were being routed through switches that were physically on American soil, eavesdropping on those calls might be a violation of the regulations and laws restricting the NSA from spying inside the United States.

But transit traffic also presented a major opportunity. If the NSA could gain access to the American switches, it could easily monitor millions of foreign telephone calls, and do so much more consistently and effectively than it could overseas, where it had to rely on spy satellites and listening stations to try to vacuum up telecommunications signals as they bounced through the air. Of course, that would mean NSA would also have direct access to the domestic telephone network as well.

Any debate within the NSA about the legalities of monitoring transit traffic became moot after 9/11. President Bush was determined to sweep away the peacetime rules that had curbed the activities of the U.S. intelligence community since the 1970s, and he readily agreed to give the NSA broad new powers. The Bush administration's answer has been to place the NSA right into the middle of the American communications bloodstream by giving the agency the secret "trapdoors" into the switching system. One outside expert on communications privacy who previously worked at the NSA said that the United States government has recently been quietly encouraging the telecommunications industry to increase the amount of international communications traffic that is routed through American-based switches. It appears that at least one motive for doing so may be to bring more international calls under NSA scrutiny.

According to government officials, some of the most critical switches are in the New York area, a key intersection between the domestic and international telecommunications networks. Switching facilities in the region feed out to telecommunications cables that dive into the Atlantic Ocean bound for Europe and beyond. The NSA now apparently has access into those switches, allowing it to monitor telecommunications traffic as it enters and exits the United States.

In addition, the NSA has the ability to conduct surveillance on the e-mail of virtually any American it chooses to target. One of the secrets of the Internet is that its infrastructure is dominated by the United States, and that much of the world's e-mail traffic, at one time or another, flows through telecommunications networks that are physically on American soil. E-mail between Germany and Italy, for example, or Pakistan and Yemen, is often routed through America. The secret presidential order has given the NSA the freedom to peruse that international e-mail traffic—along with the e-mail of millions of Americans.

In the Program, the NSA is eavesdropping both on transit traffic—calls from one foreign location to another that are routed through the United States by international telecommunications systems—and on telephone calls and e-mail between people inside the United States and others overseas. Officials who defend the Program claim that the NSA tries to minimize the amount of purely domestic telephone and Internet traffic among American citizens that it monitors, to avoid violating the privacy rights of U.S. citizens. But there is virtually no independent oversight of NSA's use of its new power. With its direct access to the U.S. telecommunications system, there seems to be no physical or logistical obstacle to prevent the NSA from eavesdropping on anyone in the United States that it chooses.

NSA also claims that it is eavesdropping only on people suspected of having links to terrorism, but there is no way to confirm exactly who in the United States is being monitored by the agency. According to officials familiar with the NSA operation, it was launched in 2002 after the CIA began to capture high-ranking al Qaeda operatives overseas. At the time of their capture, the CIA also seized their computers, cell phones, and personal phone directories and flew them to the United States for examination.

As the al Qaeda operatives began to fall into American hands, their seized laptops, cell phones, and directories led to the discovery of telephone numbers and e-mail addresses of people with whom they had communicated all around the world. The CIA turned those names, addresses, and numbers over to the NSA, which then began monitoring those numbers, as well as the numbers of anyone in contact with them, and so on outward in an expanding network of phone numbers and Internet addresses, both in the United States and overseas.

In the Program, the NSA determines, on its own, which telephone numbers and e-mail addresses to monitor. The NSA doesn't have to get approval from the White House, the Justice Department, or anyone else in the Bush administration before it begins eavesdropping on a specific phone line inside the United States. Instead, it has set up its own internal checklist to determine whether there is "probable cause" to begin surveillance. The Bush administration argues that the NSA checklist substitutes for the determination of probable cause in a court of law, but neither federal prosecutors nor other Justice Department attorneys even review the case of a suspect before the NSA begins to listen to his or her phone lines. Occasionally, top Justice Department officials audit the NSA program, but the NSA unilaterally decides on whom to spy. Bush's executive order gives the NSA broad latitude to decide what might constitute a suspicious phone number or e-mail address.

The existence of the Program has been kept so secret that senior Bush administration officials have gone to great lengths to hide the origins of the intelligence it gathers. When the NSA finds potentially useful intelligence in the U.S.-based telecommunications switches, it is "laundered" before it is widely distributed to case officers at the CIA or special agents of the FBI, officials said. Reports are said not to identify that the intelligence came from intercepts of U.S.-based telecommunications.

Bush administration officials offer conflicting information about whether intelligence gathered from the warrantless wiretaps is being used in criminal cases inside the United States. One senior administration official insisted that it never has been used in a criminal trial, but other top officials argued that the eavesdropping program has proved valuable in domestic terrorism investigations. Actually, both statements may be true. It appears that the NSA wiretaps are being used to identify suspects in the United States. But because the intelligence based on the warrantless wiretaps would almost certainly not be admissible in an American court, it is possible that the Bush administration is not attempting to take those cases to trial. Several high-profile terrorism-related cases since 9/11 have ended in plea bargains and out-of-court settlements; few have actually gone to trial. One reason for that legal strategy may be that the administration is fearful of getting caught conducting illegal surveillance operations.

The government has a number of ways to cover up the NSA's role in the domestic surveillance of people inside the United States. In some instances, the government seeks FISA court approval for wire-taps on individuals who have already been secretly subjected to war-rantless eavesdropping by the NSA.

The Bush administration justifies that procedure by saying that the government obtains search warrants if it wants to eavesdrop on the purely domestic telephone calls—between two phones inside the United States—of the individuals under surveillance through the NSA program. Since the NSA is supposed to focus on international "transit traffic" and telephone calls and e-mail messages between someone in the United States and someone overseas, government of-ficials say that they seek FISA warrants when they decide to go fur-ther to monitor all of the communications of an individual suspect.

But that process of obtaining a search warrant is clearly tainted. The Bush administration is obtaining FISA court approval for wire-taps at least in part on the basis of information gathered from the earlier warrantless eavesdropping. The government is apparently following that practice with increasing frequency; by the estimate of two lawyers, some 10 percent to 20 percent of the search warrants is-sued by the secret FISA court now grow out of information gener-ated by the NSA's domestic surveillance program.

Bush administration officials say that the NSA is using the Pro-gram to conduct surveillance on the telephone and e-mail communi-cations of about seven thousand people overseas. They also acknowledge that the NSA is targeting the communications of about five hundred people inside the United States. Each one of those indi-viduals is likely to make several phone calls and send several e-mails each day, which could mean that the NSA is eavesdropping on thou-sands of telephone calls, e-mail messages, and other communications inside the United States on a daily basis. Over time, the NSA has cer-tainly eavesdropped on millions of telephone calls and e-mail mes-sages on American soil.

The expansion of NSA's role from spying on foreigners to con-ducting domestic surveillance has implications that are sure to provoke objections from civil liberties advocates. Even some senior officials within the administration have raised questions about the Program's legality. Government officials who were aware of the surveillance program "just assumed that something illegal was going on," said one Justice Department official. "People just looked the other way because they didn't want to know what was going on."

Some senior Bush administration officials learned the outlines of the NSA operation but were never officially briefed and were stunned that the White House and Justice Department would approve the domestic spying. "This is really a sea change," said a former senior law enforcement official who questioned both its legal and public-policy aspects. "It's almost a mainstay of this country that the NSA only does foreign searches."

After President Bush signed the secret order authorizing the NSA eavesdropping operation, the Bush administration quietly notified the chief judge on the secret FISA court that approves national security wiretaps. That judge was then–U.S. District Court Judge Royce C. Lamberth, a genial, rotund Texan and a Republican. The administration didn't ask for his approval, and he didn't stand in the way when the government decided not to seek search warrants for the NSA program.

The NSA operation was scaled back, at least briefly, in the spring of 2004 when the federal judge who succeeded Lamberth as chief of the FISA court raised questions about how the NSA program was being used to generate intelligence. The concerns raised by District Court Judge Colleen Kollar-Kotelly clearly rattled the Bush administration. One official said he believed that the Program was effectively halted for about three weeks. Other top administration officials suggested that they abandoned some of the most aggressive techniques used in the NSA surveillance operation after the judge complained.

Some congressional leaders have been notified about the Program, but only in extraordinarily secret fashion and only in ways that guarantee they feel constrained from raising objections to it. Even when one lawmaker did secretly raise concerns, he was ignored by the White House. In 2002, soon after the NSA operation began, top congressional leaders from both political parties were brought to Vice President Dick Cheney's White House office and were briefed about it by Cheney, Hayden, and then–CIA director George Tenet. The congressional leaders, including Democratic Senator Bob Graham of Florida and Republican Senator Richard Shelby of Alabama, at the time the chairman and vice chairman of the Senate Select Committee on Intelligence, respectively, were not permitted to bring staff members to the meeting and were told not to discuss the matter with anyone else. It was difficult for the congressional leaders to ask any questions about the Program, because they were unable to ask their staff to do any research or oversight of the NSA operation. The congressional leaders apparently knew only what Cheney and other top administration officials told them about the Program.

Later, after new lawmakers took over the intelligence committees, only one congressional leader, Senator Jay Rockefeller, a Democrat of West Virginia, raised any concerns with the White House. After he was first briefed on the matter in early 2003, Senator Rockefeller wrote a letter to Cheney saying that he was troubled by the NSA operation and its potential for the abuse of the civil liberties of American citizens.

Rockefeller told the White House in advance that he was planning to write the letter raising objections. In response, he was told by administration officials that he had to write the letter himself. Rockefeller followed the directions and handed over the letter, but there is no evidence that he ever received a response from Cheney.

The few other Democrats who have been briefed on the operation have fallen into line with the White House, perhaps intimidated by the broad public support for tough counterterrorism measures following 9/11. But at least one other senior Democrat who was briefed later regretted accepting the administration's decision to launch the operation and realized that the White House had trapped the congressional leaders. By giving the lawmakers secret briefings with no staff present and then demanding that they never discuss the matter with anyone, the congressional leaders were paralyzed. As time wore on, it became increasingly difficult for Democrats to protest the operation, since the White House could argue that they had been receiving briefings for years and had barely complained.

One government lawyer said he went to a congressional official in 2004 to reveal what he knew about the NSA eavesdropping operation because he believed that it was unconstitutional. But nothing happened as a result of his congressional contacts. He did not know that congressional leaders had already been notified.

Apart from the very small number of senior senators and congressmen who have been briefed by the White House on the NSA program, most members of Congress believe that FISA ended, once and for all, the right of the government to conduct secret wiretaps inside the United States without search warrants or court approval. Some experts in national security law say that past presidents have periodically—and very quietly—asserted that despite FISA, they reserved the right to order warrantless wiretaps in the United States under extreme circumstances for national security purposes. But that never became an issue with Congress in the past, because until now, no president has ever actually exercised that authority since FISA became law.

The legal opinions supporting the NSA operation followed secret deliberations over expanding the NSA's role. For example, just days after the September 11, 2001 attacks, John Yoo, a Justice Department lawyer in the Office of Legal Counsel, wrote an internal memorandum that argued that the government might use "electronic surveillance techniques and equipment that are more powerful and sophisticated than those available to law enforcement agencies in order to intercept telephonic communications and observe the movement of persons but without obtaining warrants for such uses." Yoo noted that while such actions could raise constitutional issues, in the face of devastating terrorist attacks, he wrote, "the government may be justified in taking measures which in less troubled conditions could be seen as infringements of individual liberties."

But that was not an argument that the Bush administration wanted to test openly in Congress. Seeking congressional approval was viewed as politically risky because the proposal would be certain to face intense opposition from civil liberties groups. In order to support the White House decision not to seek new legislation to support the NSA operation, administration lawyers secretly argued that new laws were unnecessary because the post-9/11 congressional resolution on the war on terror provided ample authorization.

In the end, the administration's justifications for the NSA domestic surveillance operation fail to explain adequately why it would not be possible to conduct surveillance of terrorist suspects with court-approved search warrants under the FISA rules. Several government officials said they have not had any trouble obtaining search warrants for wiretaps from the FISA court since the September 11 attacks. The number of warrants approved by the court doubled between 2001 and 2003, when more than 1,700 foreign intelligence warrants were executed, according to the Justice Department. The government has also not had any difficulty in keeping those court-approved wiretaps secret. In the most sensitive cases, the wiretap requests can be handled under such tight security that knowledge of them is restricted to the highest levels of the executive branch on a need-to-know basis.

During the public debate over the Patriot Act, Bush administration officials noted reassuringly that the legislation would not expand the powers of the NSA, as if to underscore their argument that privacy concerns over the Patriot Act were being exaggerated by critics of the legislation. Even Yoo made the point, in an op-ed piece in the *Wall Street Journal*, that the Patriot Act's critics had a cartoonish view of the law. "Civil libertarians would have us believe that the Patriot Act allows CIA and NSA agents to roam freely through the country detaining anyone they please," Yoo wrote. "Nothing could be further from the truth."

One of the most worrisome aspects of the NSA's move into domestic surveillance is that it appears to be part of a broader series of policies and procedures put in place by the Bush administration that threaten to erode civil liberties in the United States. Across the administration, many questionable actions taken in the heat of the moment after the September 11 attacks have quietly become more permanent, lowering the bar on what is acceptable when it comes to the government's ability to intrude into the personal lives of average Americans. For example, in 2002 the U.S. military expanded its role inside the country with the creation of the new Northern Command, the first military command in recent history that is designed to protect the U.S. homeland. The creation of Northern Command has already raised the specter of military intelligence agents operating on U.S. soil, permanently developing new links with local law enforcement agencies, particularly those near large military bases. Few objections have been raised.

Since the Program was instituted, Hayden has been rewarded by President Bush. In 2005, Hayden was named deputy director of national intelligence, making him the top lieutenant to John Negroponte, the director of national intelligence, the top intelligence post created by the post-9/11 intelligence reforms. During his Senate confirmation hearings for his new position, Hayden was never asked publicly about the NSA's covert domestic intelligence program.

In private, he has been defensive about his role in domestic spying. Hayden has said that the operations being conducted by NSA are "legal, appropriate, and effective" as part of the war on terrorism. He has little else to say, other than that the matter is "intensely operational." The Program was still active in late 2005, several officials said.

3

CASUS BELLI

TWO KINDS OF TROUBLE developed inside the American national
security apparatus under George W. Bush. One came because
the president personally and directly authorized new operations, like
the NSA's domestic surveillance program, that almost certainly
would never have been approved under normal circumstances and
that raised serious legal or political questions. The second kind of
trouble came because of the fevered climate created throughout the
government by the president and his senior advisors. Bush sent
signals of what he wanted done; without explicit presidential orders,
the most ambitious got the message. Decision making was short-
circuited. It was this climate that influenced the handling of detainees, eroding the standards for the humane treatment of prisoners
that had guided the United States throughout its modern history.

But there were other, equally troubling ways in which Bush indirectly transformed the national security bureaucracy. The event that,
more than any other, prompted this warping was the Iraq war. It pit-
ted the Defense Department against the CIA, and factions within the
CIA against one another. Eventually, war fever spread down
through the ranks.

* * *

At the very highest level, the personal relationship between the leaders of the Department of Defense and those of the Central Intelligence Agency during the first few years of the Bush administration was fine. Quite smooth, actually.

Secretary of Defense Donald Rumsfeld and CIA Director George Tenet met regularly throughout much of President Bush's first term, over lunch at the Pentagon with only a few aides in attendance, and the two got along amicably. Tenet never developed the kind of warm and friendly relationship with Rumsfeld that he enjoyed with President Bush, or even with Secretary of State Colin Powell—like Tenet, a product of New York City—but perhaps that would have been asking too much.

One of the biggest reasons that the Tenet-Rumsfeld relationship was so cordial was that Tenet seemed intimidated—or at least outmaneuvered—by Rumsfeld and rarely challenged him on festering problems between the Pentagon and the intelligence community. Tenet and Rumsfeld would sometimes chat about the latest White House meetings they had both attended, or Tenet would regale Rumsfeld with stories and anecdotes culled from current spy cases in the Directorate of Operations, the CIA's clandestine espionage arm. Yet Tenet avoided raising some of the most pressing issues that officials at the CIA and other intelligence agencies desperately felt needed to be resolved with the secretary of defense, who, after all, controlled roughly 80 percent of the U.S. intelligence community's budget. Before each lunch, Tenet's aides would prepare a list of talking points, covering problems to be addressed with Rumsfeld, but Tenet would often ignore the list and skip over the tough issues. If Tenet asked Rumsfeld for help on a particular problem that could not be ignored—spy satellite programs, for example—Rumsfeld would usually give it to him, but Tenet seemed to press only on issues that he knew would not lead to conflict. Tenet had no appetite for waging bitter and drawn-out interagency battles, particularly against an experienced, heavyweight infighter like Rumsfeld, who had been secretary of defense for President Gerald Ford when Tenet was still an undergraduate at Georgetown. Perhaps he thought it was better to humor Rumsfeld with colorful storytelling, and stand clear of his wrath, than get down and dirty with him over turf battles that Tenet was doomed to lose.

Rumsfeld enjoyed Tenet's company. (Although at one lunch, Rumsfeld personally upbraided Tenet in front of several others for using the f-word while a woman was present, leading to a few awkward moments, according to someone who was present.) Yet at the end of some of these sessions, there was a sense, at least on the Defense Department side, that the lunch hadn't accomplished much of substance. On these occasions, after Tenet and his aides departed, Rumsfeld would turn to an aide and ask about the relevance of the spy tales and other intelligence-related anecdotes that Tenet had just spun out for him.

Did I need to know that stuff? Rumsfeld would ask.

No, Mr. Secretary, you didn't would be the reply.

"George would spend most of the time telling him anecdotes. He would talk to him about operational stuff from the DO, like 'This guy is talking to that guy,' telling him names and places," recalled one Rumsfeld aide. "Tenet was trying to impress him," one former Tenet aide acknowledged.

George Tenet was hardly the only senior official in the Bush administration to be intimidated and buffaloed by Don Rumsfeld. Early in the Bush administration, Rumsfeld made it clear that he didn't plan on taking orders from the National Security Council at the White House; he worked for George W. Bush, not Condoleezza Rice or her subordinates. If the president wanted him to do something, he could say so himself. On the NSC staff, there soon developed a strong belief that Rumsfeld had told his aides at the Pentagon that they too could ignore directions from the NSC. Eventually, it became clear that Condoleezza Rice could not rein in the Pentagon in order to get its leadership to adhere to the normal interagency processes that kept Washington running on track. It also became clear that Rumsfeld and his top aides were not paying a price for flouting the White House on key policy issues.

The dominant power relationship was between Rumsfeld and Vice President Dick Cheney, who in effect was the president's real national security advisor. Rumsfeld had been Dick Cheney's mentor and boss long before the younger man became vice president. To others in the administration, mystified by the process—or lack of a process—it eventually became evident that Cheney and Rumsfeld had a back channel where the real decision making was taking place, and that larger meetings were often irrelevant. The result was that the Bush administration was the first presidency in modern history in which the Pentagon served as the overwhelming center of gravity for U.S. foreign policy.

"Condi was a very, very weak national security advisor," observed one former NSC staffer who worked for her. "She did seem close to the president, but that really didn't translate into having control over the process. The NSC process in this administration has been dysfunctional. You had a set of principals who were polarized on almost every issue. That means you either have to forge a consensus or tee up options and make decisions. And your job as NSC advisor is to get the president to make decisions. But she let the dysfunction and lack of consensus continue. Rumsfeld was subject to no adult supervision by the national security advisor."

A former top CIA official agreed. "I think Rice didn't really manage anything, and will go down as probably the worst national security advisor in history. I think the real national security advisor was Cheney, and so Cheney and Rumsfeld could do what they wanted."

After 9/11, the structural problems in the Bush administration came into much sharper focus, leading to radical and sudden shifts in American foreign policy. Under normal conditions, new policy initiatives undergo months, if not years, of study and deliberation in the government's national security apparatus. Cabinet departments and other agencies, often with very different institutional interests, get to have their say on how to shape new proposals, and interagency meetings are held to hash out differences. Congressional leaders often have input, as do lobbyists for major industries, and sometimes even ambassadors from foreign countries that might be affected. In the process, compromises are made and sharp edges are smoothed. If things go well, by the time a proposal gets to the president and his most senior advisors, it tends to represent something close to a consensus, and policy gets forced toward the center.

The national security bureaucracy is maddeningly slow, lacks creativity, and is risk averse. It is ill suited to fight a nimble enemy in a war on terrorism. That is clear to anyone who reads *The 9/11 Commission Report,* which describes how proposals to deal with al Qaeda languished in bureaucratic hell during the Clinton administration and in the first few months of the Bush administration. Yet this creaking process does serve one purpose: it tends to weed out really stupid or dangerous ideas, unethical and even immoral ideas, ideas that could get people killed or could even start wars.

After 9/11, the moderating influences of the slow-moving bureaucracy were stripped away. The president and his principals—Don Rumsfeld, Colin Powell, Condi Rice, and a handful of others—held almost constant, crisis-atmosphere meetings, making decisions on the fly. Instead of proposals gradually rising up through the normal layers of the government, they were introduced and imposed from above. Debate was short-circuited. Interagency reviews of new initiatives were conducted on the run. The bureaucracy fell far behind the political leadership on a wide array of policy initiatives. During the eighteen months between the September 11 attacks and the March 2003 invasion of Iraq, the bureaucrats never caught up.

In that intense atmosphere, the political leaders within the administration with the clearest answers and the greatest certainty and the most persistence were quickly able to dominate the agenda. It was a perfect environment for Dick Cheney—and Don Rumsfeld.

Rumsfeld's ascendancy led to endless headaches and personnel turnover, particularly at the NSC. Rumsfeld, for example, concluded that he didn't have to pay any attention to the counterterrorism coordinator at the White House, since he believed that fighting the global war on terrorism was his job. Rumsfeld even wrote a memo to President Bush saying that he thought the job of counterterrorism coordinator at the NSC shouldn't exist and that he believed that the position was actually unconstitutional, according to former NSC officials familiar with the issue. The president may not have agreed with Rumsfeld's interpretation of the Constitution, but the defense secretary was successful in severely limiting the power and influence of the NSC over military, counterterrorism, and even intelligence matters. It was no coincidence that, after 9/11, White House counterterrorism coordinators came and went with dizzying speed; the job was eventually downgraded and merged with that of the White House coordinator for homeland security matters.

"There were many times the Pentagon just did what it wanted, no matter what the NSC said," said one former White House aide. An effective network of officials with long-standing ties to Cheney, some neoconservative, others simply conservative, scattered throughout key jobs in the administration, provided crucial support to Rumsfeld. It was Rumsfeld's force of personality, his willingness to act as an enabler for the neoconservatives within the Department of Defense and elsewhere in the administration, combined with the enthusiastic support he received from Cheney, that did so much to break down the normal checks and balances in the national security apparatus.

If Rumsfeld was willing to ignore the president's national security advisor, then why not ignore the director of the CIA? In fact, when it came to intelligence matters, it seemed as if Rumsfeld had sized up Tenet and had decided that he could run right over him. "George Tenet liked to talk about how he was a tough Greek from Queens, but in reality, he was a pussy," complained one former Tenet lieutenant, roughly. "He just wanted people to like him." So when Rumsfeld began to propose a series of initiatives that directly challenged Tenet's power and influence over the intelligence community, particularly after 9/11, it was not very surprising that Tenet shrank back—or that the White House was absent from the field of bureaucratic battle.

Rumsfeld had come into office eager to reform the hidebound Pentagon. Transforming the military was to be Rumsfeld's signature issue, and among his projects he included the maze of military intelligence agencies that were components of the Department of Defense. He told aides that, when it came to intelligence, he "wanted one dog to kick"—meaning that he wanted a top advisor who could streamline and consolidate the Pentagon's sprawling intelligence empire and help him bring it under his direct control. Years before President Bush and Congress finally agreed in the heat of the closing days of the 2004 presidential campaign to create a new "Director of National Intelligence," Rumsfeld was eagerly drawing up his own unilateral reorganization of the intelligence bureaucracy. The difference was, of course, that his plans called for the consolidation of power over the intelligence apparatus within the Office of the Secretary of Defense. There was no need for a new Director of National Intelligence when the nation already had Don Rumsfeld.

Rich Haver, the man who had worked behind the scenes to try to get Tenet ousted during the Bush transition, was now Rumsfeld's top intelligence aide. He was placed in charge of the reorganization effort, which immediately raised red flags at the CIA.

Rumsfeld's plan for "one dog to kick" turned into a proposal to create an intelligence czar within the Pentagon who would oversee all intelligence agencies in the Defense Department budget, including the National Security Agency, the National Imagery and Mapping Agency (later renamed the National Geospatial-Intelligence Agency, which processes and analyzes spy satellite photography), the Defense Intelligence Agency, and the intelligence arms of each major military service. That meant just about everything in the intelligence community, except the CIA and the State Department's small intelligence branch.

Rumsfeld told Haver that he wanted to make certain that Tenet accepted the plan. Rumsfeld said it couldn't just be something that Tenet acquiesced to, but it actually had to be something he approved. So Haver took the plan to Tenet, and the CIA director responded flatly that "it looks as if you are trying to do my job," as Haver recalled. Haver dutifully went back and modified the proposed reorganization, scaling back the degree to which it cut into the CIA director's control over the collection of intelligence from spies, spy satellites, and listening posts. Haver took it back to Tenet, and this time the CIA director gave his blessing.

Tenet refused to resist any further, despite loud cries from members of his senior staff and even from Brent Scowcroft, the former national security advisor in the first Bush administration who was serving as the chairman of the President's Foreign Intelligence Advisory Board. Scowcroft had known Rumsfeld for thirty years, since the Nixon and Ford administrations, and he knew better than almost anyone else in modern Washington how Rumsfeld operated. Scowcroft felt sure that this was just the start of Rumsfeld's empire building. Scowcroft also saw Rumsfeld's initiative as a direct assault on the traditional role of the director of central intelligence. Ever since the CIA was created by the National Security Act of 1947, the CIA director has had two distinct jobs—one as the head of the CIA, and the other as the overall boss of the entire intelligence community, made up of some fifteen agencies. This second function had always been ill defined, mainly because the budgetary power of the director of Central Intelligence did not extend much beyond the CIA, and without control over the purse strings, it was hard to issue orders to other agencies.

Since most of the intelligence budget was buried within Pentagon spending, it was critical that the CIA director work well with the defense secretary. In the past, that had usually not been a major problem for the CIA director, because the secretary of defense almost always had more important things to worry about than the 10 percent or less of the Pentagon budget that involved intelligence matters. There had, of course, been disputes, but in modern history, there had never been a secretary of defense who also lusted after the job of director of central intelligence. At least, not until Rumsfeld.

Tenet refused to heed Scowcroft's warnings. Former aides say that Tenet never showed much interest in intelligence reform or reorganization. His top priorities were maintaining a strong relationship with the president and running the Directorate of Operations. Tenet rarely expressed much interest in efforts to coordinate the entire intelligence community. In the end, he didn't object to the legislation creating Rumsfeld's one dog to kick, otherwise known as the undersecretary of defense for intelligence. The only surprise was that Haver didn't get the job. He had made many enemies, and in the end was perhaps better suited to the role of agent provocateur than that of manager of a large bureaucracy. The job went instead to Rumsfeld's most trusted aide, Stephen Cambone, who had earlier been staff director of Rumsfeld's Commission to Assess Ballistic Missile Threat to the United States. (In his newly created position, Cambone would eventually become an even more controversial figure than Haver, and would face questions about his role in the development of policies concerning the U.S. military's handling of detainees in Iraq.)

Rumsfeld's desire to gain control over intelligence only intensified after 9/11, when he watched, aghast, as the CIA took the lead in Afghanistan, while the military was painfully slow to gear up for war there. Rumsfeld didn't want to take a backseat again and, with Cambone at his side, began pushing for more aggressive activities by U.S. Special Forces and the even more secretive and elite special operations teams in the Joint Special Operations Command. In Afghanistan, CIA paramilitary personnel had joined with Special Forces and Special Operations units to marry intelligence to muscle and firepower. Rumsfeld seemed to believe that, in the future, there was no reason the Pentagon couldn't handle such covert activities all by itself. There was also no reason that its operations had to be limited to combat zones, such as Afghanistan or even Iraq. Rumsfeld believed that the Pentagon should create clandestine teams that would be free to operate anywhere he chose. In the global war on terrorism, the entire world was a combat zone, and secret U.S. activities in otherwise peaceful and nonthreatening countries could be justified as "preparation of the battlefield."

Rumsfeld's plans represented a radical expansion of the Defense Department's existing espionage capabilities. The Defense HUMINT (Human Source Intelligence) Service, a wing of the Defense Intelligence Agency, had for years done some limited clandestine intelligence work, but it had never been involved in the kind of high-risk operations that Rumsfeld had in mind for the secret units that he created. Unlike the clandestine service of the CIA, Rumsfeld's new covert units—given the benign-sounding name of "operational support elements"—didn't fall under the government's existing rules governing covert action, rules that required explicit presidential authorization and congressional notification. In fact, the Defense Department didn't seem to believe its special teams needed to tell anyone else in the government what they were doing, let alone coordinate their activities with the American ambassadors and CIA station chiefs in the countries in which they were planning to operate. Rumsfeld was creating his own private spy service, buried deep within the Pentagon's vast black budget, with little or no accountability.

Before long, the State Department and CIA began to hear reports from ambassadors and station chiefs that special covert military teams were operating in Africa and elsewhere in the third world. In some cases, the embassies discovered their activities only by accident or at second hand. Whenever CIA officials complained to the Pentagon, they were told that the failure to notify them of the operations was an oversight and that the teams were simply conducting reconnaissance.

The new cowboys at the Pentagon were clearly asking for trouble. In early 2005, trouble came: members of an operational support element team working in Latin America killed a man outside a bar. The American personnel then failed to report the incident to the U.S. embassy for several days. The incident has never been made public, but several officials familiar with the matter say it raises serious questions about the degree to which the Pentagon's new secret teams are being properly managed.

While Rumsfeld pushed and pressured the CIA on covert operations after 9/11, Deputy Defense Secretary Paul Wolfowitz and other neoconservatives at the Pentagon, and their allies in the office of Vice President Dick Cheney, pushed and pressured the CIA on the toxic issue of Iraq. Just as Tenet failed to stand up to Rumsfeld, he and his management team failed to act as a buffer against the pressure being brought to bear by the administration's hard-liners.

If the rest of the administration was eager to take on Saddam Hussein, the post-9/11 climate was completely different at the CIA, where the war against Osama bin Laden was all-consuming. If there was one other long-term threat that worried the agency's leadership, it was not Iraq, but Iran, with its burgeoning nuclear weapons program and its close ties to terrorist organizations like Hezbollah.

"It is hard for people outside the agency to understand how little we were thinking about Iraq," recalled one top intelligence official. The CIA's lack of focus on Iraq—and in particular, the agency's failure to see Saddam Hussein as an imminent threat to the United States—infuriated the administration's hard-liners. They believed that the opportunity for war with Iraq presented by the attacks on

New York and Washington could best be exploited by linking Baghdad to 9/11. Failing that, it might be possible to tie Iraq more generally to al Qaeda.

The problem for the hard-liners was that the CIA was the keeper of the vast majority of classified intelligence on al Qaeda, and the agency's analysts had seen no evidence of Iraqi involvement in 9/11 and had no conclusive proof of a terrorist alliance between Saddam Hussein and Osama bin Laden. Those answers did not satisfy Wolfowitz, or his equally certain lieutenant, Undersecretary of Defense for Policy Doug Feith.

Wolfowitz had a long history of challenging CIA assumptions that went against his beliefs. In the 1970s, he had been a member of the original "Team B," which savaged the CIA's estimates of the Soviet nuclear threat, and in the 1990s, he had been a member of Rumsfeld's ballistic missile commission, which was critical of the CIA estimates of the strategic threat posed by rogue states such as North Korea. In each case, Wolfowitz had found that the agency had not been sufficiently hawkish, and now, in the aftermath of 9/11, he once again found that the CIA was being soft, this time on the possibility that Saddam Hussein was behind the attacks on the United States. Wolfowitz felt that there "was intellectual dishonesty in the intelligence community," recalled one former Pentagon official. As Wolfowitz listened to intelligence briefings from CIA analysts on al Qaeda after 9/11, he angrily concluded that they were not even considering alternative possibilities that included Iraqi involvement. The CIA was an arrogant, rogue institution, he believed, unwilling to support administration policy makers.

Israeli intelligence played a hidden role in convincing Wolfowitz that he couldn't trust the CIA, according to a former senior Pentagon colleague. Israeli intelligence officials frequently traveled to Washington to brief top American officials, but CIA analysts were often skeptical of Israeli intelligence reports, knowing that Mossad had very strong—even transparent—biases about the Arab world. After each Israeli briefing, the CIA would issue reports that were circulated throughout the government, but they often discounted much of what the Israelis had provided. Wolfowitz and other conservatives at the Pentagon became enraged by this practice; they had begun meeting personally with top Israeli intelligence officials and knew which elements of the Mossad briefings the CIA was downplaying. "And so Paul got angry," said one former Pentagon official.

Wolfowitz personally complained to Tenet about the CIA's analytical work on Iraq and al Qaeda, telling the CIA director that he didn't believe the agency's analysts were approaching the issue with open minds. "George would say that he would fix it, and that he understood," recalled a former top Pentagon official. "And I'm sure halfway back between the Pentagon and Langley he would say, 'Oh, that's just Wolfowitz, forget it.' And I'm sure the analysts at the CIA were all just saying, fuck Wolfowitz. So Paul set up his own unit to look at it. And then that really pissed off the people at the CIA."

Former colleagues believe that Wolfowitz felt enormous personal guilt over the failure of the first Bush administration to topple Saddam Hussein at the end of the first Gulf War in 1991. At the time, Wolfowitz was in the defense policy post that Feith later held, and he had privately opposed the decision to stop the war after the liberation of Kuwait. But he chose not to push hard to change the policy, and his guilt over that failure eventually seemed to turn to obsession, Wolfowitz's former colleagues believe. And so Wolfowitz and the like-minded Feith created a special intelligence unit, known as the Counter-Terrorism Evaluation Group, to sift through raw intelligence reports, searching for ties between Iraq and al Qaeda. The group was set up in Feith's office; its real purpose was to serve as a Team B for the neoconservatives at the Pentagon, a counterweight and rival to the CIA in the struggle to shape intelligence on Iraq.

The Pentagon leadership also turned increasingly to the Iraqi exile Ahmed Chalabi and his Iraqi National Congress (INC) for information—a move that was another direct challenge to the CIA, which had long since proclaimed that Chalabi, who had been a CIA asset in the early 1990s, was unreliable. The CIA and Chalabi had suffered a very bitter divorce following the collapse of the CIA's covert action programs against Iraq in the mid-1990s, in which Chalabi had played a leading role.

In the aftermath of the 1991 Gulf War, the first President Bush had authorized the CIA to launch a covert campaign to undermine Saddam Hussein's regime, but none of the operations the agency conducted over the following decade ever offered a glimmer of hope of forcing Saddam from power. The CIA's covert action plans in the 1990s left behind a trail of blown operations and exposed agents. Saddam's security apparatus thoroughly penetrated the CIA's operations with double agents and always seemed at least one step ahead. Within the CIA, the Iraq covert action program came to be seen as a black hole, where careers went to die. The fastest-rising case officers stayed away. Over the years, as the CIA's best Iraqi agents inside the country came in from the cold and defected to the West, the agency failed to replace them by recruiting new spies. Intelligence operations against Saddam Hussein were allowed to atrophy.

Whatever his faults, Chalabi had an unerring sense of how to play the Washington power game, and after George Bush was elected he smartly launched an all-out charm offensive on the neoconservatives and their congressional Republican allies. Chalabi had known Richard Perle and a few other conservative figures for many years, and now they came to his aid, at least in part because of a shared hatred of the Clinton White House—and the CIA.

The Clinton administration, like the CIA, had flirted with Chalabi and rejected him. In 1998, under pressure from congressional Republicans, Clinton had agreed to the Iraq Liberation Act, calling for the United States "to support efforts to remove the regime headed by Saddam Hussein." In addition, the government created a special program to pay Iraqi exiles, including Chalabi's Iraqi National Congress, for information about Saddam's regime. The information collection program was at first administered by the State Department, but officials there felt the same about Chalabi as did their counterparts at the CIA, and the program withered. With the State Department anxious to rid itself of Chalabi, the Pentagon eagerly snapped up the information collection program in 2002, and it was turned over to the Defense HUMINT Service, under the watchful eyes of Paul Wolfowitz and the Pentagon's civilian leadership. Chalabi had found a home.

But it wouldn't do much good to have Chalabi on the Pentagon's payroll if the CIA constantly raised objections, particularly if the agency's analysts tried to cast doubts on the credibility of intelligence reports provided by Iraqi defectors introduced to the United States government by Chalabi and his organization. So from the earliest days of the Bush administration, the White House pushed the CIA to drop its long-standing opposition to Chalabi. "They sent us that message a thousand times, in a thousand different ways," said one former senior CIA official.

One former White House official saw how the message was delivered, even before 9/11. In a White House meeting in the spring of 2001 to discuss new proposals on how to undermine the Iraqi regime of Saddam Hussein, Deputy National Security Advisor Stephen Hadley admonished Deputy CIA Director John McLaughlin, saying that the CIA had to get over its dislike of Chalabi and stop bad-mouthing him, so that the United States could work with Chalabi to overthrow Saddam. According to the former White House source, McLaughlin made it clear to Hadley that the CIA wouldn't stand in the way and passed the White House message back to CIA management.

The White House pressure had an impact. The CIA still refused to work directly with Chalabi, and Tenet personally warned Wolfowitz in White House meetings to be careful in his dealings with the Iraqi exile. But the CIA did not try to stop the Pentagon from distributing intelligence reports based on information from Iraqi defectors, including some provided by the INC. The result was that the information from the Iraqi exiles was injected directly into the intelligence community's bloodstream as the United States was gearing up for war in Iraq.

As the pressure mounted within the Bush administration to topple Saddam Hussein, some senior CIA officials went to George Tenet to explicitly voice their concerns that war with Iraq would hurt the ongoing battle against terrorism, former officials say. There was a strong belief among counterterrorism officials within the agency that an invasion of Iraq would distract attention and resources away from the ongoing fight against al Qaeda just when the terrorist group seemed to be on the ropes. The agency would be stretched too thin if it had to handle both Afghanistan and Iraq, a number of officials, including James Pavitt, the deputy director of operations of the CIA, believed.

Tenet's response was never satisfying.

"A lot of people went to George to tell him that Iraq would hurt the war on terrorism, but I never heard him express an opinion about war in Iraq," said one former Tenet aide. "He would just come back from the White House and say they are going to do it." That was the central message that Tenet brought back to the CIA from the White House and the Pentagon: war with Iraq was inevitable, and it was time for the CIA to do its part. Agency officials who appeared to be unenthusiastic about Iraq soon mysteriously found themselves sidelined, while their more eager and ambitious colleagues began to rise, both within the Directorate of Operations and in the Directorate of Intelligence, the analytical arm. The pressure from the Bush administration was being transmitted directly into the ranks of the nation's intelligence community, affecting careers and lives.

* * *

In April 2002—nearly a year before the invasion of Iraq—CIA case officers stationed all over Europe were ordered to attend a special conference in Rome, during which officials from the CIA's Iraq Operations Group casually told the assembled CIA officers that Iraq had been on the Bush agenda from the very beginning.

"They said this was on Bush's agenda when he got elected, and that 9/11 only delayed it," said one CIA officer who attended the conference. "They implied that 9/11 was a distraction from Iraq. And they said Bush was committed to a change of leadership in Iraq, and that it would start with kinetic energy—meaning bombs. Meaning war."

The Iraq Operations Group, once considered a backwater where managers sent deadwood, was now taking center stage. To their skeptical colleagues in the rest of the CIA, the IOG officers now seemed to have evolved into ambitious—and dangerous—advocates for war. Much of the conference was taken up by presentations from the IOG staff about the evils of Iraq, most of it publicly available information about Saddam Hussein's past atrocities and his ambitions for weapons of mass destruction. The presentation was so rudimentary, and the tone was so bellicose, that one source who attended thought the conference was like a secret "pep rally" to build support within the skeptical CIA for the war. "We were supposed to go out and tell our liaison contacts how bad Saddam was."

One of the key ideas floated in the Rome conference was for the CIA to launch a propaganda campaign all over Europe, to try to plant stories in the European media in support of war with Iraq, according to the source who participated in the meeting. The CIA is prohibited from trying to plant propaganda in the media in the United States, but there are no legal restrictions against its propaganda efforts overseas. Today, of course, with the Internet and the globalization of the media, it would be nearly impossible to guarantee that false information planted overseas would not make its way into the American press. It's unclear how extensive any such propaganda efforts were in Europe. The opposition to the invasion throughout the Continent suggests that if the CIA did launch a propaganda campaign, it was utterly ineffective.

Meanwhile, the intense focus on Iraq on the part of the highest-ranking Bush administration officials soon became clear to CIA officers in the field, even though they were far removed from the hothouse atmosphere in Washington. It is well known that Vice President Cheney repeatedly visited CIA headquarters to meet with agency analysts and other officers during the run-up to the war, posing sharp questions about the CIA's analytical reports about Iraq. But what is not known is his direct intervention in CIA field operations, in an effort to prod greater effort against Saddam Hussein and his regime.

The CIA's espionage operations in Western Europe had been badly crippled in the 1990s by a series of failed operations and flaps, most notably a spy scandal in Paris in 1995. The agency had become far more cautious in Western Europe as a result, and only rarely conducted "unilateral" operations without the cooperation of the intelligence service of the local country. That was the case in the Netherlands; the CIA did little there that the Dutch did not know about and approve. That was a problem when it came to operations related to Iraq, because the Netherlands was strongly opposed to the Bush administration's plans for war. The CIA wanted to "pitch"—to try to recruit to become an American spy—an Iraqi intelligence officer operating out of Holland. But the Dutch were so opposed to the Bush administration's approach to Iraq that the Dutch intelligence service refused to allow the agency to try to recruit the Iraqi in Holland.

Vice President Cheney took an interest in the case, and over a weekend called the prime minister of Holland to ask him to intervene personally, to approve the operation targeting the Iraqi official. The prime minister rebuffed Cheney. Still, the fact that the vice president of the United States was willing to intervene directly in a relatively minor espionage case was a signal that the White House expected much more aggressive action from the CIA on Iraq.

In November 2002, CIA station chiefs from all over the Middle East gathered in London for a secret meeting at the United States Embassy. They had been summoned by senior CIA officials from headquarters to a conference inside the CIA station spaces in Grosvenor Square. This was to be a come-to-Jesus meeting, one in which officials from headquarters would make it clear that it was time for the skeptics among them to drop their reluctance to engage on Iraq. War was just a few months away.

Of course, the official position of the Bush administration was that it was still open to all diplomatic options and that war with Iraq was not inevitable. At the United Nations, the bitter debate between the United States and Europe over Iraq was still playing out before the television cameras. But the troops could not sit in Kuwait forever.

The officials from headquarters were clearly on board with the coming war. But there was also a sense, at least among some officials with the CIA's Iraq Operations Group, that many CIA officers in the field, including many of the station chiefs in the Middle East, were not enthused about the looming invasion. That sense of division and internal conflict prompted the meeting, according to one former official from the Iraq Operations Group.

"First, it is useful to highlight why the London meeting was called," the former IOG official, who attended the London meeting, recalled. "After several worldwide cables from IOG, the Near East front office, and the DDO's office, we found little movement in the field on the Iraq issue.

"Many of the field managers were steeped in past practices, unimaginative, uninspiring, and risk averse. IOG mounted relentless pressure on the field to attack the Iraq CA [covert action] and FI [foreign intelligence] taskings aggressively, but little activity of substance followed. We did succeed in assembling a long list of naysayers and enemies over the course of two years. This lack of movement on the Iraq target triggered the call by the ADDO [the assistant deputy director of operations] for the London meeting."

Several officials who attended the conference recalled that the introductory message at the London meeting from the senior officials from CIA headquarters to the station chiefs was simple: The game is on. We are going to war in Iraq. There will be no further debate on the issue. And it is time for each station chief to talk plainly with their liaison contacts in the foreign intelligence services of their host countries and inform them that it is time to join in, time for the Arab world to cooperate with the Americans on Iraq.

The former IOG officer who attended recalled that the NE Division station chiefs made it clear they were still unenthusiastic and offered "excuses on why they didn't want" to get involved with Iraq and the CIA's covert plans.

Many of the NE Division station chiefs put it differently. They saw the IOG officers as pro-war zealots who were finally having their day in the sun thanks to the Bush administration. The tensions between the two sides continued throughout the London conference—and throughout the prewar period. The former IOG official acknowledged that there was a deep divide before the war between CIA officials involved with Iraqi matters and other officials in the agency's Near East Division. "We kept saying that the president has decided we are going to war, and if you don't like it, quit."

During the conference, an Iraq Operations Group official began to discuss the agency's covert plans for sabotage to undermine the Iraqi regime. During the discussion of sabotage, someone in the conference floated an idea that left some of the gathered CIA station chiefs shocked and stunned.

The former IOG official recalled in detail the discussion about sabotage in the London conference. "We made sure everyone understood, we would be conducting sabotage activities," the former official recalled. "Most agency officers have never been involved in any direct action, simple, subtle or direct sabotage activities, or a successful covert action program." The chief of IOG "introduced the topic of sabotage in the context of both internal and external targets, specifically commenting on the multiple avenues used by the regime to bring in cash, sensitive regime goods, and items of interest to Saddam and his family. The task was to interdict this flow and cause the regime to question the loyalty of those involved in the process. We were never under the illusion that Saddam would feel pain by what we did. The object of the effort was part of a multifaceted effort to cause dissension, distrust, and exacerbate the paranoia within the regime's inner circle.

"One of the key avenues of shipment for illicit goods was the gulf ferry that funneled goods from Sharja, Dubai, and other gulf ports to Um Qasr."

According to the former IOG official, when the role of the ferry was described, a young station chief spoke up, recommending that the agency "should sink the ferry." The chief of IOG then "commented that the ferry and the interdiction of inner circle personal materials was a legitimate target, but sinking the ferry was not an option because it carried people as well as freight. A discussion ensued regarding access to the ferry in port, which ports might afford access, which liaison services might be willing to allow access, options using assets to affect unilateral access, and if a sabotage technique or material could be introduced on the ferry that would cause a mechanical failure and force the ferry to remain in port, thus preventing its continued use by the regime," the former IOG official recalled. He stressed that "at no time was there any serious discussion about sinking the ferry."

Two CIA station chiefs who attended the conference recalled the discussion about the ferry, but left the meeting with the impression that the IOG had been considering sinking a ferry in order to make it a casus belli against Baghdad. The two CIA sources who recalled the ferry discussion said that they could not understand how this action could have provided a justification for the invasion.

The ferry discussion left some of the senior CIA officers in the audience shocked, uncertain if they had heard correctly. A third station chief who attended the conference but who did not recall the ferry discussion observed that there was a feeling within the CIA that people involved with Iraqi issues "were under intense pressure from management and DOD and policy makers to find a way to kick-start the war. They presented some radical and cockamamie ideas about how things could go."

There is certainly no evidence that any sabotage against a ferry was ever carried out. The two sources who reported that the plan was under consideration say they never heard anything further about the proposal and don't know what became of it. They also say that top CIA officials were not in the room during this part of the presentation and they do not know whether any top CIA officials or senior Bush administration policy makers ever heard of the idea.

During the conference, the IOG officials went on to describe several other covert action proposals then under consideration. To the senior CIA field officers, all with extensive experience in the Middle East, the ideas seemed feckless. Among other things, the plans included equipping low-level Iraqi agents with special spring-loaded darts that they could use to destroy the windshields of cars owned by members of the Iraqi regime. Large supplies of the darts were later delivered to forward CIA stations, but nothing was ever done with them. (The former IOG official who attended the meeting said that the CIA did have its agents conduct some acts of sabotage, including the derailment of a train just days before the invasion.)

After the London presentation, a group of station chiefs went out for drinks at a nearby pub and a few them quietly spoke among themselves about what they had just heard. One officer spoke up and said he had never heard of the ferry idea before and said that it would never happen as long as he had anything to say about it, according to one of the station chiefs who attended the London meeting and who was also at the pub afterwards.

Other station chiefs who attended wondered what games were being played. Were midlevel guys just throwing out wild ideas?

"What it told me was that they didn't have any serious plans for covert action and they were just grasping at crazy ideas," said one of the CIA station chiefs who attended the London presentation and recalled the discussion of the ferry idea. "I think they had nothing else, they had no real intelligence to offer, and they were desperate to be in the game with the military."

If such ideas were discussed in London, it may have been due in part to the fact that the CIA had so few assets in Iraq and so few options. It takes years to develop and recruit well-placed spies, particularly inside closed regimes. When George W. Bush entered office and Iraq was suddenly a top priority again, the CIA's cupboard was bare. The CIA had access to parts of northern Iraq through the Kurdish zone, but its only sources in southern Iraq were low-level Iraqi agents, smugglers who could go back and forth between Iraq and Kuwait to provide firsthand impressions of conditions in Iraq, and some who were willing to take sample swabs near suspected WMD sites and bring them back to the CIA for testing.

One CIA officer said that he reviewed the agency's restricted handling files on Iraq in the summer of 2002, covering the most sensitive cases and operations being conducted. He was shocked by what he found—or rather, didn't find. "RH is the most closely held stuff. I thought I was going to read about spies that no one knew about. But they had nothing. No agents anywhere close to the regime, or to the WMD programs, or the security services. Zero. All they had were these plans for covert action. Sabotage and these fantasies they had. But they had no intelligence. That was why they came up with these silly covert-action ideas, because they had nothing else."

The CIA's lack of agents inside Iraq didn't matter in the last years of the Clinton administration, when Iraq was falling off the White House priority list. But it suddenly represented a major problem as the Bush administration began to ratchet up its rhetoric to make the case for war in 2002 and early 2003. Did Iraq have WMD or didn't it? How close was Saddam to building a nuclear weapon?

Despite the obvious shortcomings in the agency's intelligence on Iraq, the CIA's top leaders convinced themselves that they knew the answers. But at least a few at the agency weren't so sure. They became deeply concerned by the new willingness of CIA management to ignore the warning signs.

4

THE HUNT FOR WMD

D OCTOR SAWSAN ALHADDAD was very busy when she received the strange phone call. She was so busy, and the call was so strange, that she wasn't quite certain whether to follow up. It was May 2002, and the caller said he was from the CIA and that he wanted to meet with her. He didn't sound crazy, but she wasn't sure.

A quiet, petite, olive-skinned woman in her fifties, Sawsan wondered why a CIA officer who said he was calling from Pittsburgh would want to talk to an anesthesiologist in Cleveland.

Curiosity finally got the better of her. Fear got to her, too; old fears of police and security men that had receded gradually over the last two decades, as she and her husband had built a wonderful new American life, with a beautiful daughter, in a plush and sprawling home, in one of Cleveland's most luxurious outer suburbs. Sawsan thought she had left her fears behind when she and her husband escaped from Iraq in 1979, lying to their bosses at the hospital in Baghdad about their plans for a brief vacation in London. It was before anybody in America had given much thought to Saddam Hussein, back before the United States thought much about granting Iraqi exiles political asylum from a mad dictator. Eventually, they managed to rebuild their lives and become American citizens.

Sawsan decided to check out the mysterious caller before agreeing to meet him. She found someone at the FBI's Cleveland field of-

fice who would listen to her story. Was there such a person in Pittsburgh working for the CIA? Sawsan was surprised when the FBI
agent called her back. He had checked with FBI headquarters in
Washington, and it turned out that the man in Pittsburgh was real,
and the call was genuine. The CIA really did want to talk to Dr.
Sawsan Alhaddad of the Cleveland Clinic. So she finally agreed to
meet with "Chris" from Pittsburgh.

As Chris was trying to contact Sawsan Alhaddad, it was becoming clear that President Bush was determined to invade Iraq. In his
2002 State of the Union Address the previous January, Bush had
warned of an "axis of evil," of which Iraq was one of only three members. Bush and his aides charged that Saddam Hussein was a threat
to the United States because he possessed weapons of mass destruction and because his regime harbored terrorists. Saddam might use
his weapons against America, or give them to terrorists to do the job
instead. In either case, an attack with chemical, biological, or nuclear
weapons would make September 11 look like child's play. It was a
risk, George W. Bush said, that a post-9/11 United States was not
willing to take.

Throughout that spring, the Bush administration had been
steadily ratcheting up the rhetoric about the threat posed by terrorists, weapons of mass destruction—and Iraq. Vice President Dick
Cheney went on television to say he was "almost certain" of more terrorist attacks on the United States, while Secretary of Defense Donald Rumsfeld announced that it was only a matter of time before
terrorists would get weapons of mass destruction from rogue states
like Iraq. In late May, Bush spoke in Berlin, where he warned that
once terrorists obtained chemical, biological, or nuclear weapons
from countries like Iraq, "no inner voice of reason, no hint of con-
science would prevent their use." With the war in Afghanistan wind-
ing down, George Bush's Washington was inexorably turning its
attention toward Baghdad.

Sawsan told Chris that it was not possible for her to meet with him right away. Her mother had come to Cleveland from Iraq for advanced treatment for colon cancer, and Sawsan had to care for her. Maybe they could talk later, she told the CIA man. In June, Sawsan's mother died, and the Iraqi woman was buried in the American heartland. Soon, Sawsan was ready for the CIA.

The White House drumbeat on Iraq and weapons of mass destruction kept building that summer. It was filling the front pages and the airwaves by the time Chris finally sat down with Sawsan at a Cleveland Starbucks in early August. The president and his lieutenants insisted that no decision about whether to invade Iraq had been made, but in a major foreign policy speech at West Point in June, Bush had forcefully made the case for taking preemptive action against dictatorships such as Iraq that harbored weapons of mass destruction. "Containment is not possible when unbalanced dictators with weapons of mass destruction can deliver those weapons on missiles or secretly provide them to terrorist allies," Bush told the graduating class at West Point. "We cannot defend America and our friends by hoping for the best. We cannot put our faith in the word of tyrants, who solemnly sign nonproliferation treaties and then systemically break them. If we wait for threats to fully materialize, we will have waited too long." By July, the Pentagon's plans for an invasion of Iraq had leaked to the press, and it was becoming more difficult by the day for Bush to hide his intentions. Inside the government, meanwhile, more secret documents were written to bolster the case against Iraq. On August 1, the CIA issued a classified paper that was distributed to senior Bush administration officials. It concluded that a shipment of high-strength aluminum tubes from China to Iraq was a sign that Iraq was reviving its uranium enrichment program in order to build an atomic bomb.

Chris stunned Sawsan when he explained why he had come to talk to her. He told her that she could help in President Bush's new war on terror. She could help by going to Baghdad on a secret mission for the CIA. Chris explained that the CIA wanted Sawsan, a middle-aged mother from Cleveland, to travel to Iraq and become a spy.

The CIA had identified Saad Tawfiq, Sawsan's brother, a British-trained electrical engineer living in Bagdhad with his wife and three children, as a key figure in Saddam Hussein's clandestine nuclear weapons program. The CIA knew who he was, Chris told Sawsan, but it didn't have any way to try to talk to him. So the CIA wanted Sawsan to go to Baghdad to talk to her brother and see if he would be willing to defect, through the Kurdish zone in northern Iraq. The CIA couldn't help him cross into the Kurdish zone, but if he got there on his own, the CIA could get him out to the West. If he wasn't ready to defect, the CIA wanted Sawsan to ask him a series of questions about Saddam Hussein's efforts to build nuclear, chemical, and biological weapons. The CIA was convinced that Saad Tawfiq knew the most sensitive secrets about Iraq's weapons programs and that he might be willing to tell his sister the truth about Saddam Hussein's ambitions.

Sawsan found it hard to believe that the CIA didn't have some other way to get information out of Baghdad. But after thinking hard about it, she decided she was willing to do her part. She had not seen her brother since 1989, on a brief and nervous visit to pre–Gulf War Iraq, but she thought he might want to help. She told Chris she was willing to try.

Sawsan was volunteering for a late, desperate Hail Mary pass by the CIA. As President Bush and other administration officials were turning up the rhetorical heat on Iraq, key leaders within the CIA faced an uncomfortable fact: the United States did not have the proof to back up what the president was saying publicly about Iraq and its weapons of mass destruction. Worse, the CIA had been operating virtually in the blind about Iraq for years. Its evidence was either old and obsolete, or from secondhand, thirdhand, or fourthhand sources, defectors and exiles who had their own political agendas. Almost every analyst at the CIA *assumed* that Iraq had WMD—but they didn't have hard evidence to back it up. What was worse, many of them knew it.

In 1998 the United Nations had withdrawn its weapons inspectors from Iraq after a showdown with Saddam Hussein over access to key sites in the country. President Bill Clinton launched a four-day bombing campaign to punish Iraq for its refusal to cooperate with the UN inspectors, but the bombs had no real effect. The withdrawal of the inspectors severely hampered the CIA's ability to keep track of Iraqi weapons efforts in the years before the 2003 war. Throughout the 1990s, the CIA had relied almost entirely on the UN inspectors for intelligence about Iraq's weapons programs. After their withdrawal, the CIA failed to develop reliable sources of its own inside Iraq to report on Baghdad's weapons programs.

In the year before the 2003 war, the CIA had only one case officer spying from inside Baghdad. He was posing undercover as a diplomat working in the embassy of another country. But that case officer did not develop or recruit any sources who knew the status of Iraq's weapons programs. The agency had also developed sources within the Iraqi military, largely through the Iraqi National Accord, an exile group led by Ayad Allawi (a CIA asset who later became the interim prime minister of Iraq), but none of those military officers had any firsthand knowledge about Iraqi WMD. By mid-2002, most of the agency's information was at least four years out of date.

Charlie Allen, the CIA's assistant director for collection and a legendary figure within the agency, was the highest-ranking CIA official willing to try to do something about the problem. Allen had carved a unique niche for himself within the U.S. intelligence community. He looked for collection "gaps," intelligence targets that were not being adequately covered by the CIA and other intelligence agencies. He realized that Iraqi WMD represented an enormous intelligence gap.

While other top CIA officials, including CIA Director George Tenet and Deputy Director for Operations James Pavitt, dithered and failed to mount any serious operations to get more spies into Iraq to find out what was going on, Allen, an old hand who had little time for Tenet and the circle of yes-men and yes-women on Tenet's senior staff, began a renegade effort to search for new sources of information.

He pushed for several new collection programs, including one that called for approaching members of the families of Iraqi scientists who were believed to be involved in secret weapons programs. At the time, the CIA had no direct access to key Iraqi scientists, and so using family members as intermediaries to find out what the scientists were doing seemed like the next best thing. Most of the key scientists who had been involved in the weapons programs in the past had been interviewed repeatedly by UN inspectors during the 1990s. During those earlier interviews, they had all insisted that the weapons programs had been abandoned. But the United States was convinced that the scientists had been lying, since they were always closely watched by Iraqi security during the interviews. At least, thanks to the UN inspections, the CIA had a fairly comprehensive list of Iraq's senior weapons scientists. Charlie Allen realized that list gave him something to go on.

Allen's collection team began contacting family members living outside of Iraq, asking them whether they would be willing to help the agency by going back to Iraq to talk to their relatives about their scientific work. At least thirty relatives of Iraqi scientists agreed to cooperate, including Sawsan Alhaddad. The CIA was eager to get her on board. Saad Tawfiq had long since been identified as one of the senior figures in the Iraqi nuclear program. He was a Shia Muslim, never completely trusted by the Sunni-dominated regime of Saddam Hussein, yet Saad was one of the true technical experts that Iraq couldn't do without. The CIA had initially contacted his younger brother, who was living in Houston. After he rebuffed them, Charlie Allen's team approached Sawsan in Cleveland.

Throughout August 2002, Chris became a regular in Cleveland, meeting Sawsan at restaurants and at her home in suburban Moreland Hills, finally bringing a CIA technician along to train Sawsan in the rudiments of espionage. The agency had put together a long list of questions she was to ask her brother, but Sawsan couldn't just walk into Bagdhad carrying a memo from the CIA. So the technician tried to teach her the art of secret writing, showing her how to read and write using invisible ink on fast-burning paper. Sawsan was a practical woman, and she realized that the CIA's techniques were too cumbersome and dangerous if done incorrectly in the heart of Iraq. She finally told Chris she would skip the secret communications and would memorize the questions instead. Privately, she decided to use her favorite crossword puzzles to guide her. She wrote mnemonic aids into crossword puzzles that she could take with her on the plane to Iraq, key words to remind her of the questions she was supposed to ask.

Before sending Sawsan, the CIA wanted to make certain that her brother would be willing to talk with her once she got there. Sawsan offered the perfect intermediary to get word to him. Her mother-in-law was visiting Cleveland from Baghdad and was due to return home in early September. She could tell Saad that the CIA wanted to talk to him through Sawsan, and could ask him if he would do it.

Frightened but willing, the mother-in-law agreed, returned home to Baghdad, and found a moment to talk to Saad on the street outside his home, away from the listening devices that were almost certainly planted inside.

They want to talk to you, and they will send Sawsan, the old woman told Saad Tawfiq. *Sawsan will call you tonight, and ask how you are feeling. If you are willing, tell her that you are okay.*

Sawsan called her brother, asked him how he was feeling, and he said that he was okay. She repeated the question three times to make certain that she heard him right.

Sawsan left for Baghdad a few days later, explaining to Iraqi authorities that her mother had just died and that she needed to settle her estate. Since she was now carrying an American passport with her married name (which was different from the family name on her old Iraqi passport) it didn't register with the Iraqis that this was the same woman who had escaped so many years before.

It was early September. The Bush administration was now raising the stakes on Iraq, warning that Saddam Hussein's nuclear weapons program posed an immediate threat to the United States and the White House was strongly suggesting that war could not be delayed. On September 8, National Security Advisor Condoleezza Rice coined a memorably ominous phrase on a Sunday talk show when she said, "while there will always be some uncertainty about how quickly" Saddam Hussein can acquire nuclear weapons, "we don't want the smoking gun to be a mushroom cloud." Just as Rice was making the public case against Iraq, the Defense Intelligence Agency issued a classified report entitled "Iraq's Reemerging Nuclear Weapons Program," which concluded that Baghdad was on its way to building the bomb. Vice President Cheney, sounding impatient with any further debate, went on a Sunday talk show to add that "this problem [Iraq] has to be dealt with one way or another."

To ratchet up the pressure, the Bush administration leaked information to the American press. The *New York Times* published a story on September 8—the same day Rice issued her mushroom cloud warning—making public the evidence that Iraq had acquired aluminum tubes to rebuild its nuclear weapons program. The story stated that "More than a decade after Saddam Hussein agreed to give up weapons of mass destruction, Iraq has stepped up its quest for nuclear weapons and has embarked on a worldwide hunt for materials to make an atomic bomb, Bush administration officials said today."

*   *   *

When Sawsan stepped off the plane at Saddam International Airport
in Baghdad, she didn't even recognize her brother. When they finally
spotted each other, it was a joyous reunion. Saad had a friend in the
Iraqi security services, and he helped Sawsan sail through the Iraqi
customs and immigration bureaucracy. On the ride into town,
Sawsan could also barely recognize the city of her youth, Baghdad
had changed so dramatically. She was surprised to see that so many
women were now covered. Baghdad didn't seem as secular and open
as it once did.

They returned to Saad's house—it had been their parents' home
in the old days—in the affluent Mansour neighborhood of Baghdad,
located right next door to the headquarters of the Mukabarat, the
Iraqi intelligence service. Sawsan was depressed to see that years of
war and privation had led to the steady deterioration of their family
home. It had been damaged repeatedly in U.S. bombing raids targeting the neighboring Mukabarrat building, both in the first Gulf War
in 1991 and in a 1993 raid to punish the Iraqis for trying to kill the
first President Bush. She spent her first day catching up with family
and old neighborhood friends, then waited until late the second
night of her visit to speak privately with her brother.

Until that night, she had never really had a candid conversation
with her brother about his work in Iraq. She had seen him only twice
in twenty-five years. He had been allowed to come to the United
States once in 1983 for a professional conference, and she had returned once to Iraq, in 1989 for a medical convention. On that visit,
Sawsan had noticed that her mother was unhappy and worried that
her son was involved in work that might get him hurt, but Saad had
refused to talk about it. They had tried to keep in touch since, but it
had been difficult, and so her brother's life was something of a mystery to her.

* * *

Saad Tawfiq's entire career on the inside of one of the most ruthless regimes in modern history, his life as a key member of the most secretive scientific team in the world—the team that tried to build a nuclear bomb for Saddam Hussein—had hinged on one moment, a moment when he was forced to choose between freedom and family responsibility.

He was raised a son of privilege and standing in old Iraq, an Iraq in which family and education meant something, before it was twisted and corrupted by Saddam Hussein. Born in 1951, Saad was the son of a doctor and spent much of his youth in the southern Iraqi city of Basra until he was sent away to boarding school in Baghdad. There, he attended the finest prep school Iraq had to offer, Baghdad College, run by American Jesuit priests from Boston College. In college Saad first met many of the boys who would later run Iraq. The American Jesuit teachers instilled in Saad Tawfiq a hunger for learning. He also learned to play baseball and basketball, and he gained a glimpse at the wider world of possibilities beyond his Arab homeland. It didn't matter to him that he was a Muslim Shia attending a Catholic school.

From Baghdad College, Saad went to Baghdad University to study engineering, and his academic prowess landed him a graduate fellowship at the University of Sussex in Britain. Throughout the late 1970s, he worked on his doctorate at Sussex and lived in Brighton with his Iraqi wife and growing family. It was an idyllic time, when all things still seemed possible. His PhD thesis in electrical engineering, in his specialty of systems and control, dealt with optimizing the control of harbor cranes for rapid ship unloading, a supremely practical issue that allowed him to dream of transforming his hometown, the harbor of Basra, into a world-class port.

Saad completed his thesis and received his doctorate in August 1980. He had been in Britain for four years, and Iraq increasingly seemed like part of his past. He was quickly offered two different jobs by Western firms doing business in the Middle East, and accepted one from a British firm handling the construction and air-conditioning of tunnels in Saudi Arabia that were to be used by Muslim pilgrims on the path of the Haj to Mecca.

In January 1981, he was all set to move to Liverpool and start his new career when he received word that his father had died in Baghdad. Four months earlier, Iraq had invaded revolutionary Iran. The brutal war between the two neighbors was already chewing up the Iraqi Army and giving Saddam Hussein an enormous appetite for fresh troops. Even though Saad was now a thirty-year-old scientist with a wife and child, a return trip to Iraq now meant an almost certain ticket into the army. But Saad was the oldest son, and his mother was now alone. His two sisters and his younger brother had all escaped to the United States. For Saad, there really was no choice—he had to return. He knew it meant the end of his dreams of a life beyond Iraq.

As soon as he returned, Saad was dispatched into the army, but before long a friend told him of a unique job opportunity, one that could gain him an exemption from further military service: the Iraqi Atomic Energy Commission was looking for new scientists. There was an added fillip—a free parcel of land, courtesy of Saddam Hussein.

By mid-1981, Saddam Hussein had already become desperate to find new weapons that could break the grim calculus of war with Iran, and he was enamored of the terrible possibilities offered by weapons of mass destruction. The centerpiece of his efforts was a French-designed nuclear reactor then under construction in Tuwaitha, just south of Baghdad. The reactor was part of a larger complex that included a second, smaller French reactor and a Soviet-made test reactor that was already in use. Once the plant was completed with the help of French engineers, Saddam Hussein hoped the reactor would bring him one step closer to turning Iraq into a nuclear power. Although the French had not provided Iraq with the technology to use the reactor to reprocess weapons-grade fuel, that was clearly Saddam Hussein's ultimate objective.

Saad Tawfiq was told nothing about a weapons program when he was hired. Instead, he was assigned to a series of scientific research projects, none of which had anything to do with bomb making. Yet on June 7, 1981, the day before Saad Tawfiq was due to start work, the Israeli air force bombed the Tuwaitha plant in a stunning and high-risk raid by F-15 and F-16 fighters. The French reactor, known to the outside world as Osirak but called Tammuz 1 by the Iraqis, was destroyed. The Israeli government of Prime Minister Menachem Begin announced that it had conducted the raid in order to block Saddam Hussein from obtaining an atomic bomb with which he could destroy Israel.

Paradoxically, it was the Israeli strike on Tuwaitha that led Saad Tawfiq into the clandestine world of nuclear weapons development. As Saad and others dug through the rubble at Tuwaitha, trying to salvage whatever equipment they could, Saddam Hussein began searching for a new path to nuclear weapons. Finally, a scientist under house arrest offered the regime a solution. Ja'afar Dia Jafar, a Shia who had fallen out of favor with Saddam, said that he knew of a way to develop a bomb without a large reactor. He said Iraq could follow the original path of the American Manhattan Project, which built one of its first bombs using a technique that was later abandoned because it was so slow and tedious, and required enormous amounts of electricity. But those problems were offset by two advantages. The old Manhattan Project technique would be hard for the outside world to detect, and better still, much of the Manhattan Project's technology was now in the public domain and would be relatively easy for Iraq to duplicate.

Jafar was describing a uranium-enrichment process known as EMIS—electromagnetic isotope separation—which calls for the use of large magnets to help separate ions of two different uranium isotopes. EMIS can produce weapons-grade material in a relatively straightforward manner, and it can do so without the use of a modern nuclear reactor. Of course, EMIS still wouldn't be easy for a small country like Iraq. "The Americans had eleven Nobel laureates to do EMIS during the Manhattan Project—we had none," recalled Dhafer Rashid Selby, who was a top manager in the Iraqi program working for Jafar. But EMIS was such a slow, labor- and energy-intensive process that every other nuclear power in the world had abandoned it. No one in the West would ever guess that Iraq was now secretly using it.

Jafar's proposal was adopted, and he was released from house arrest in order to create a new EMIS program. One of the first people he tapped to join his new team was Saad Tawfiq. Before long, Saad would become one of Jafar's protégés. He followed his lead throughout the rest of his career and eventually became one of his senior managers.

The nuclear program was given a cover name—Petro-Chemical 3—to convince outsiders that the team was involved in oil-related work. No one, not even Jafar, ever came to Saad and told him he was now assigned to work on a nuclear bomb. Even within the team, there were no explicit orders announcing the bomb program. The team just came together and began working, with subgroups assigned to very specific tasks. Left unsaid was the fact that the only end result that could come from the combination of all of the specific tasks of all of the various subgroups was the creation of an atomic weapon. "It was unspoken; no one ever said it was a weapons program," recalls Saad. "We would talk about the subsystems we were working on, about magnets, power supply, but we wouldn't talk about the overall program, even though it was obvious to everyone. We would sometimes talk among ourselves about it, but we couldn't talk openly." Saad never even told his wife any details about his work.

At the time, Saad didn't have any qualms about trying to help

Iraq build the bomb. He believed that it would help create an "equilibrium with Israel," he recalled. "And I didn't think Saddam was a madman."

A key source of nuclear technology for Jafar's new team was the United States itself. In fact, Jafar had recommended using the EMIS process in part because so much old American technological information was publicly available. A major breakthrough for the team came in 1982, when Imad Khouri, the head of information programs for Jafar's team, traveled to the United States and obtained Manhattan Project designs for EMIS from public sources in American libraries. When Khouri returned to Baghdad, Saad Tawfiq and the other scientists were given Manhattan Project data related to their subsystems.

Saad came to the United States to obtain crucial data as well. In 1983, he attended a professional conference in Houston and joined the Instrumentation Society of America, which issued instrumentation standards critical for Saad's systems. With his membership in the ISA, the organization regularly shipped Saad dozens of books and sophisticated software packages produced in the United States that helped him mechanize the design procedures his team was working on.

By 1987, the EMIS program was working just as Jafar had hoped—Iraq was slowly making progress in uranium enrichment, and Jafar's team had developed several prototypes of EMIS separators. There were some glitches, particularly when Jafar insisted that the team deviate from the processes used by the Manhattan Project. Still, they had managed to work for six years without anyone outside the regime detecting their operation, certainly not the International Atomic Energy Agency, the Israelis, or even the Americans.

Despite the later fears and suspicions of the CIA, Iraq did not need to buy uranium from Niger in order to provide fuel for a bomb. Early on, Jafar's team relied on small amounts of uranium furnished by the Italians in the late 1970s. Later, a small quantity of uranium was purchased from Brazil. Once Jafar's team was ready for full-scale production, there was plenty of uranium in Iraq. It was extracted from a phosphate-mining region known as Akashat. To handle the natural uranium, Jafar's team built a uranium purification plant in a hilly area thirty kilometers west of Mosul, and began mining uranium in the Akashat region in the early 1980s. Later, before the second Gulf War, when Saad Tawfiq heard the allegations of Iraqi uranium purchases from Niger, he knew that the "information did not come from anyone in Iraq who knew anything."

Throughout the mid-1980s, a string of facilities related to the EMIS process were clandestinely constructed, giving Iraq a large nuclear infrastructure that the West had still not detected. But in late 1987, Saddam Hussein, evidently impatient with the slow pace of the project, placed his thuggish son-in-law, Hussein Kamel, in charge of the nuclear program. Kamel saw the nuclear program as the crown jewel in the regime's WMD efforts, but his demands to accelerate the program, creating new teams to enrich uranium through more advanced means, ultimately backfired. The Iraqi campaign to obtain dual-use technology for the more advanced techniques demanded by Kamel attracted unwanted international attention and suspicion. "We had always wanted to do things indigenously, but Hussein Kamel thought you should just go out and buy what you need," recalled Saad. Two of Hussein Kamel's men were arrested at Heathrow Airport after trying to buy American nuclear triggers. Jafar's effort to mask the program was unraveling.

It was Saddam Hussein's decision to invade Kuwait in 1990 that proved to be the fatal mistake. The nuclear program had become a major enterprise, with at least eight thousand workers. Yet it was still two to three years away from producing a weapon. Eight separators had been installed for the EMIS program, but significant enriched-uranium production was still far in the future.

If Saddam had waited to attack until the nuclear team was ready, his power and influence in the Middle East might have been secured.

But with the Kuwaiti invasion came intense and unrealistic pressure on the team to produce. Hussein Kamel ordered that they work around the clock during the long months between the time of the Iraqi invasion of Kuwait and the U.S.-led Desert Storm campaign. Saad Tawfiq spent almost every waking moment during those months at the nuclear facilities. There was discussion of trying to rig a "dirty bomb"—an explosive device stuffed with radioactive material already on hand—but the orders never came and the plan was abandoned. In the end, Jafar's team could not produce the bomb that Saddam needed to ward off the international coalition.

The end for the nuclear program came almost by accident: the Americans destroyed the Iraqi program from the air without even realizing it. In early 1991, a U.S. aircraft that had completed its raid on another Iraqi target had turned for home with two bombs left. The pilot began searching for another target to drop his remaining weapons and was directed to a complex of buildings in Tarmiya, about 30 kilometers north of Baghdad, that the United States apparently believed was part of the Iraqi Military Industrialization Commission. The pilot bombed the largest buildings in the complex and headed for home. Surveillance photos of the bomb damage intrigued American targeteers. There was unusual activity around the damaged buildings, and the Iraqi behavior at the bomb site suggested that this compound was more important than previously believed. A B-52 strike was ordered to hit it again. The B-52 carpet bombing utterly destroyed the Tarmiya uranium-enrichment facility, known to the Iraqis as the Safa factory. It effectively ended Iraq's nuclear ambitions. Jafar's program never recovered.

By May 1991, UN weapons inspectors were in Iraq trying to determine the state of Iraq's WMD programs. At the time, they still did not know that Iraq had had an EMIS program, and Saddam Hussein wanted to keep it that way. In June, Saad and other members of

Jafar's team were called in to the presidential palace and told by Jafar that the program was over and that they must now get rid of all of the evidence of its existence. "My orders were to destroy or hide all incriminating evidence, and leave only the equipment that could be shown to be dual-use technology." In the space of seventy-two frantic hours, Saad and other scientists loaded equipment onto 150 tractor-trailers and escorted them out into the western desert. The scientists tagged the equipment as best they could, but so much of it was thrown into the trucks and jumbled together that it was difficult to keep track of it all. For Saad, the worst came late one night when he and his truck convoy got lost in the desert, uncertain which way to head. Finally, the truckloads were turned over to Saddam's Special Security force to conceal and bury.

It wasn't long before the IAEA inspectors began to figure out that Tarmiya had been the site of an enrichment facility. In the summer of 1991, the Iraqi regime's lies about its past nuclear program began to unravel. Under mounting pressure, Hussein Kamel flip-flopped and ordered the scientists *not* to hide anything. "There were so many changing orders, hide everything, then don't hide anything," recalled Saad. About three months after the tractor-trailers loaded with equipment had first gone into the desert, the inspectors were shown the buried equipment. The combined force of the bombing raids during the war and the inspections afterward brought the nuclear program to a close. "The program was finished and we had no purpose in life," Saad recalled.

In March 1992, Hussein Kamel convinced Saddam to let him keep the nuclear scientists together within his organization, the Military Industrialization Commission. There, Saad and the rest of the team found themselves working on Hussein Kamel's pet industrial projects, all the while knowing that they were biding their time until the UN inspections and sanctions were lifted so they could resume their nuclear work. "Hussein Kamel's idea was to keep people together under the MIC and then see what happened," recalled Saad.

In the meantime, "we were there to work on Hussein Kamel's dreams." Any staff members from the team who left to find other work were arrested and jailed until they agreed to return to the MIC.

Yet as the inspections and the sanctions dragged on throughout the 1990s, it became less and less likely that the nuclear program could be easily reconstituted. Finally, in 1995, Hussein Kamel defected, then redefected, and was executed. The MIC and Jafar's teams drifted in his wake. Money for Saad and his team began to dry up, and the scientists had to scramble to find new projects to work on. By the time his sister Sawsan arrived in 2002, with war once again looming, Saad was still at the MIC, working to develop a nitric acid plant for fertilizer production, and was also teaching on the side at the University of Technology in Baghdad. He wasn't doing anything that could lead to the development of a nuclear bomb, because Iraq's nuclear program had been dead for more than a decade.

Sawsan could tell that her brother was very nervous about her visit and that he was reluctant to speak candidly. Despite all of Iraq's problems, he and his family had carved out a reasonably comfortable life for themselves in Baghdad. His children were in good schools, and he was reluctant to do anything to upset his family's status. "He was not into cloak-and-dagger stuff," Sawsan remembered later. He refused to take any time off from work while Sawsan was visiting, and he was clearly afraid to bring attention to the fact that his American relative was in Baghdad at a time when political tensions were so high.

When they finally were able to find time alone to talk late on that second night, Sawsan and Saad took a walk outside. She quietly told him that the CIA wanted him to defect. *They want you to get to the Kurdish zone.*

Her brother scoffed. *How can I get across to the Kurdish area? They are always watching.* It was impossible, Saad told her. Particularly since the CIA wasn't offering him any help to get out of Baghdad. As planned, Sawsan then told Saad that the CIA had given her questions to ask him about the Iraqi nuclear weapons program. How close were the Iraqis to having a nuclear warhead? How much weapons-grade fuel did Iraq already have? How advanced is the centrifuge program? What process are you using for isotope separation? Where are the weapons factories? Can you identify the scientists involved in the weapons program?

Saad Tawfiq gave his sister a look of worldly incredulity. *Where did they come up with these questions? Don't they know that there is no nuclear program?*

Sawsan was stunned. "He just kept saying there is nothing," she remembered later. The nuclear program has been dead since 1991, he explained. There is nothing left. There hasn't been for over a decade. They must know that.

Sawsan tried to continue with her list of questions, but they all seemed to Saad to be the product of some fantasy. We don't have the resources to make anything anymore, he told her. We don't even have enough spare parts for our conventional military. We can't even shoot down an airplane. We don't have anything left. If the sanctions are ever lifted, then Saddam is certain to restart the programs. But there is nothing now.

Saad told his sister that he was fed up with all the talk of war, and that maybe, between the two of them, they now had an opportunity to do something about it. Now, he was briefly starting to get energized by her visit. *Maybe if we tell the CIA that we don't have anything, no weapons, maybe there won't be another war.* Saad told his sister that he worried that America was going to invade for no reason, when there was nothing left of the weapons program. He had seen the effects of war on Iraq before, and he didn't think the country could stand another.

It was sometimes hard for the brother and sister to find time to talk privately during her ten-day stay. Saad was teaching at the university, but also had to attend meetings at night related to his primary job as a manager at Iraq's Military Industrialization Commission. Saad also had a secretary who came to his house several times while Sawsan was visiting. Only after the 2003 war did Saad discover that she was an informant for Iraqi intelligence.

One night, they couldn't arrange time alone until 2:00 A.M. Sawsan again suggested they take a walk outside. Saad said no; they would arouse suspicions, and their actions might be reported. So he unplugged the telephones and turned up the volume on the television, and they whispered to each other. Sawsan told her brother that the CIA wanted to know what he thought about information they had received from one former Iraqi scientist who had defected to the United States, and who was now telling the Americans that Iraq still had weapons of mass destruction. Saad was dismissive, saying that the guy was a phony and never knew anything. He was just saying those things to get paid.

Just before Sawsan left to return to the United States, Saad told her again that he didn't think it would be worthwhile for him to risk trying to defect. *Why take the risk,* he said, *when all I can tell them is that there is no program.* It would be up to Sawsan to carry that message back to the CIA.

Sawsan flew home to Cleveland in mid-September and was quickly contacted by the CIA, which then flew her to Washington for a series of meetings with the agency's analysts. Four CIA officers met Sawsan in a hotel in suburban Virginia, eager to debrief their agent from Iraq.

Sawsan told the CIA men that her brother was unable to answer their carefully prepared list of questions because there was no nuclear weapons program in Iraq. She explained that the defector they were relying on for information about the nuclear program didn't know what he was talking about. She said that Saad had said that even before the first Gulf War, Iraq was three years away from producing a nuclear bomb and that the program had been abandoned after the war. Saad had told her that there was no effort under way to rebuild the nuclear program. It would have been impossible to restart the program without it being noticed, he had said.

She apologized that she was unable to get specific answers for many of their detailed questions, but her brother had repeatedly told her that there simply wasn't any nuclear program.

I'm sorry I don't have more for you.

As they sat and listened to Sawsan in the Virginia hotel room, the CIA officials all nodded and seemed sympathetic. Every answer is helpful, they told her. Sawsan noticed that they didn't seem surprised that her brother had insisted that there were no weapons programs left. What about purchases of uranium from overseas? Sawsan had been told to ask Saad about the Niger shipments.

No, Saad said that was not going on, Sawsan recounted. Nothing like that was going on. In fact, Sawsan said, Saad kept wondering where the CIA was getting these crazy questions.

This is good, the CIA men repeated. All the information you brought us is good.

Sawsan's debriefing lasted a couple of hours, and then the CIA men packed up, thanked Sawsan for her time, and put her back on a plane for Cleveland. After she returned home, Chris from the CIA's Pittsburgh station came to visit again, and this time brought a small gift: a wood and glass case containing a folded American flag that he said had flown over CIA headquarters in Langley, Virginia. The CIA, he told her, wanted to express its gratitude for her bravery. Sawsan was touched, but something Chris said to her husband during the visit worried her.

We think that Saad is lying to Sawsan, Chris told Sawsan's husband. *We think he knows much more than he is willing to tell her.* To Sawsan's husband, that didn't make any sense, and he said so.

Why would he lie? What does he have to gain from it? You wanted him to defect, but he said there was no program to talk to you about.

The CIA man smiled, nodded, and left. Sawsan Alhaddad's debriefing report was filed along with all the others from the family members who had agreed to return to Baghdad to contact Iraqi weapons scientists.

All of them—some thirty—had said the same thing. They *all* reported to the CIA that the scientists had said that Iraq's programs to develop nuclear, chemical, and biological weapons had long since been abandoned. Charlie Allen's program to use family members to contact dozens of Iraqi scientists had garnered remarkable results and given the CIA an accurate assessment of the abandoned state of Iraq's weapons programs months before the U.S. invasion in March 2003.

CIA officials ignored the evidence and refused to even disseminate the reports from the family members to senior policy makers in the Bush administration. Sources say that the CIA's Directorate of Operations, which was supposed to be in charge of all of the agency's clandestine intelligence operations, was jealous of Allen's incursions into its operational turf and shut down his program and denigrated its results. President Bush never heard about the visits or the interviews.

The agency's Directorate of Intelligence, in charge of analyzing information collected by the agency's spies and other sources, did not even consider using the information from the family members. Analysts responsible for intelligence reports on Iraqi WMD never included any of it in their assessments. The reports from the family members of Iraqi scientists were buried in the bowels of the CIA and were never released for distribution to the State Department, Pentagon, or the White House. The CIA had obtained hard evidence that Saddam Hussein had abandoned his efforts to obtain weapons of mass destruction—and the agency chose not to share that information with the president of the United States, who was about to send American troops to fight and die in Iraq. Sawsan's dangerous trip into the heart of Saddam Hussein's Iraq had been for nothing. Saad

Tawfiq's desperate hope that his sister could carry a message back to the CIA that might prevent a war was dashed by the petty turf battles and tunnel vision of the agency's officials.

In October 2002—one month after Sawsan Alhaddad's trip to Baghdad—the U.S. intelligence community issued a comprehensive report, known as a National Intelligence Estimate, on the status of Iraq's weapons of mass destruction. It was supposed to be the agency's best effort to pull together everything known about Saddam Hussein's weapons programs, while providing the intelligence community's most judicious assessments of where the programs were headed in the future. It confidently stated that Iraq "is reconstituting its nuclear program."

One of the only advantages to living next door to the headquarters of the Iraqi intelligence service was good television reception. By accident, Saad Tawfiq had discovered that, with a few adjustments, it was possible for him to capture the satellite television feed as it beamed down into the intelligence headquarters next door. Since Iraqi intelligence officials were obligated to know what the world was saying about their extremely demanding boss, Saddam Hussein, they got all the Western news channels, including the BBC and CNN. Free satellite television didn't make up for the shattered windows, blown-out doors, and other collateral damage his house had suffered over the previous decade, but it was something.

From his home in Baghdad in February 2003, Saad Tawfiq watched Secretary of State Colin Powell's televised presentation to the United Nations about Iraq's weapons of mass destruction. As Powell dramatically built the American case for war, Saad sank further and further into frustration and despair.

They didn't listen. I told them there were no weapons.

5

SKEPTICS AND ZEALOTS

E VER SINCE the U.S. invasion of Iraq and the subsequent discovery that Iraq did not have weapons of mass destruction, officials in the Bush administration and the CIA have insisted that they truly believed before the war that those threatening weapons did exist. President Bush and his top advisors have repeatedly claimed that they did not exaggerate the threat, and top CIA officials have publicly argued that their ominous assessments that Iraq had ongoing chemical, biological, and nuclear weapons programs were fully justified by the available intelligence.

But in fact, many CIA officials—from rank-and-file analysts to senior managers—knew before the war that they lacked sufficient evidence to make the case for the existence of Iraq's weapons programs. Those doubts were stifled because of the enormous pressure that officials at the CIA and other agencies felt to support the administration. CIA Director George Tenet and his senior lieutenants became so focused on providing intelligence reports that supported the Bush administration's agenda, and so fearful of creating a rift with the White House, that they created a climate within the CIA in which warnings that the available evidence on Iraqi WMD was weak were either ignored or censored. Tenet and his senior aides may not have meant to foster that sort of work environment—and perhaps did not even realize that they were doing it—but the result was that the CIA caught a fatal case of war fever.

The reports from Sawsan Alhaddad and other family members of Iraqi scientists were not the only warning signs that were ignored. In fact, doubts about the quality of the intelligence on Iraq's weapons of mass destruction pervaded the ranks of the CIA before the war.

One former senior CIA officer recalls a conversation he had in December 2002 with the chief of the Counterproliferation Division (CPD) of the Directorate of Operations, the unit within the CIA that was supposed to be in charge of recruiting spies and collecting intelligence on WMD in Iraq and other countries. The division chief admitted during the conversation that the agency "didn't have much intelligence on Iraq WMD," according to the former CIA officer. "There were a lot of people who said we didn't have enough intelligence," the former officer added.

Some CIA officials who were skeptical were shunted to the side by CIA management. Alan Foley, the director of the CIA's Weapons Intelligence, Nonproliferation, and Arms Control Center (WIN-PAC), told a former colleague on the day of Secretary of State Colin Powell's UN presentation in February 2003, that the CIA simply didn't have the evidence to back up what Powell was saying to the world. This was a stunning confession from the man in charge of all of the CIA's analysis related to weapons of mass destruction. But it also was a signal that the professionals within the ranks of the CIA felt that they were being railroaded. "I talked to Foley on the day of Powell's UN speech, and he said, we just don't have it. It's not very good," a former colleague of Foley's later recalled.

Despite his high rank, Foley felt outmaneuvered within the agency's management on the issue of Iraq, his former colleague said. After the war and the failure to find any WMD in Iraq, Foley briefly came into the news as a result of a controversy between the CIA and the White House over the handling of the intelligence related to whether Iraq had tried to purchase uranium from Niger. In his 2003

State of the Union Address, President Bush referred to reports that Iraq had been trying to buy uranium from Africa as evidence that Saddam Hussein was developing nuclear weapons. But the credibility of that reporting had already come into question before the president's speech, and it was later revealed that documents about supposed uranium sales by Niger to Iraq were forgeries.

Foley was dragged into a public argument between Tenet and Condoleezza Rice over who was responsible for allowing such flawed intelligence to get into the State of the Union Address. CIA officials told reporters that Foley tried to warn NSC staffer Robert Joseph, who was handling WMD issues at the White House, against including the material in the speech; the White House said Foley never told Joseph that the information was bad. Said to be fed up and bitter, Foley left the CIA not long after that battle.

Another CIA source said that two analysts who raised questions about the reporting on Iraqi weapons programs before the war were "smacked down" by other officials in WINPAC, although the CIA source did not know what punishment the two suffered for their skepticism. The two analysts continued to work at the agency, and, according to the CIA source, they later testified about their experiences to the independent WMD commission.

By contrast, more hawkish officials, even very junior analysts, found it easy before the war to bring their reports to the attention of the CIA leadership—as long as the reports tended to confirm the existence of Iraqi weapons of mass destruction.

One former CIA official recalled how Tenet's chaotic management style allowed even inexperienced analysts to get their reports directly to the CIA director without adequate vetting by more experienced professionals. Tenet chaired daily meetings on key issues, including both Iraq and counterterrorism, and those conferences were often crowded with mid-level and junior officials eager to get noticed by the director. By presenting their reports during these large conferences with top CIA management, these junior officers were able to short-circuit the normal analytical process. Intelligence reports that seemed to corroborate the administration's agenda could thus go directly from an ambitious junior analyst to George Tenet, who could then take them straight to the White House and George W. Bush. The CIA's mistaken embrace of intelligence claiming that a shipment of aluminum tubes was proof that Saddam was reconstituting his nuclear weapons program was a prime example of that management disarray.

"I was in a meeting chaired by Tenet where you had kids from WINPAC," recalled a former official. During the meeting, the former official recalled, Deputy CIA Director John McLaughlin observed that he had heard that analysts at the Energy Department were skeptical that the aluminum tubes could be used for a nuclear program. "And this young analyst from WINPAC, who didn't look older than twenty-five, says, no, that's bullshit, there is only one use for them," recalled the former official. "And Tenet says, 'yeah? Great.'

"So you had people sprinkled throughout the organization who felt like they could go right to the top, and no one was there to contradict them."

One key nuclear weapons analyst in WINPAC, who has been identified in the press only as "Joe," was one of the primary advocates within the agency arguing that the aluminum tubes were for use in a nuclear weapons program. The CIA had almost no other physical evidence to show that Iraq was developing nuclear weapons, and so Joe's tube intelligence reports brought him high-level attention. CIA sources say Joe was often able to deal directly with McLaughlin, circumventing the normal chain of command. (The independent WMD commission later concluded that the intelligence community's failure on the Iraqi nuclear issue was perhaps the most damaging of any of its errors during the run-up to the Iraq War.)

As the invasion of Iraq drew closer, an attitude took hold among many senior CIA officials that war was inevitable—and so the quality of the intelligence on weapons of mass destruction didn't really matter. This attitude led CIA management to cut corners and accept shoddy intelligence, other CIA officials believe. "One of the senior guys in the NE Division [the Near East Division of the Directorate of Operations] told me that it isn't going to matter once we go into Baghdad, we are going to find mountains of this stuff," recalled a former CIA official, who left the agency after the war. This acceptance of weak intelligence among senior CIA officials appears to be the backstory to the famous so-called Downing Street Memo.

According to a former senior CIA official, the memo—the leaked British government document from July 2002 that provided a British assessment of the Bush administration's plans for Iraq—was written immediately after a secret conference in Washington between top officials of the CIA and British intelligence. The memo, dated July 23, reported that "there was a perceptible shift in attitude" in Washington about Iraq. The memo went on to say that "military action was now seen as inevitable. Bush wanted to remove Saddam, through military action, justified by the conjunction of terrorism and WMD. But the intelligence and facts were being fixed around the policy."

The memo reflected an assessment of the prevailing attitude inside the Bush administration offered to Prime Minister Tony Blair by Sir Richard Dearlove, the head of MI6, the British intelligence service. Just days before, Dearlove and other top MI6 officials had attended a CIA–MI6 summit meeting held at CIA headquarters, in which the two sides had candid talks about both counterterrorism and Iraq. According to a former senior CIA officer, the summit meeting was held at the urgent request of the British.

The American and British intelligence services are so close that under normal circumstances, they hold an annual summit to discuss a wide range of issues in a relaxed setting. The year before it had been held in Bermuda. But after 9/11, Tenet had told other CIA officials he was too busy to be bothered with another conference with the British, particularly one held in a remote location. The British were very insistent, however, and kept pushing for the meeting, the former CIA official said. The MI6 officials made it very clear to their CIA counterparts that they had to sit down and talk immediately.

CIA officials believe that Prime Minister Blair had ordered Dearlove to go to Washington to find out what the Bush administration was really thinking about Iraq. While Blair was in constant communication with President Bush, he apparently wanted his intelligence chief to scout out the thinking of other senior officials in Washington, to give him a reality check on what he was hearing from the White House.

"I think in hindsight that it is clear that Dearlove was insistent on having the summit because Blair wanted him to find out what was going on," said the former CIA official.

Tenet finally agreed to the conference as long as it could be held at CIA headquarters, rather than out of town. The session was scheduled for Saturday, July 20, 2002.

The two sides ended up spending most of that Saturday together. One of Tenet's great attributes was his ability to develop warm relationships with the chiefs of allied intelligence services, and Tenet had an especially good personal relationship with Dearlove. He was usually very candid with his British counterpart.

During the Saturday summit, Tenet and Dearlove left the larger meeting and went off by themselves for about an hour and a half, according to a former senior CIA official who attended the summit. It is unclear what Tenet and Dearlove discussed during their one-on-one session. Yet Dearlove's overall assessment was reflected in the Downing Street Memo: the CIA chief and other CIA officials didn't believe that the WMD intelligence mattered, because war was coming one way or another.

"I doubt that Tenet would have said that Bush was fixing the intelligence," said a former CIA official. "But I think Dearlove was a very smart intelligence officer who could figure out what was going on. Plus, the MI6 station chief in Washington was in CIA headquarters all the time, with just about complete access to everything, and I am sure he was talking to a lot of people."

The poisonous climate in the U.S. intelligence community during the prewar period was perfect for hustlers and fabricators eager, for their own reasons, to tell tall tales to the Americans. Many of them were Iraqi exiles who reported that Saddam did have WMD. There were warnings given to top CIA officials that some of the Iraqi exiles and defectors were lying, but these warnings were often ignored. Perhaps the most egregious example came in the case of an Iraqi exile who was given the apt code name of Curveball.

The information provided by Curveball was critical to the Bush administration's case that Iraq was developing biological weapons. Curveball said that Saddam Hussein's regime had developed mobile biological laboratories that enabled Iraqi scientists to keep their bioweapons out of sight of UN inspectors. Secretary of State Colin Powell relied on information from Curveball in his presentation to the United Nations in February 2003.

Later, the independent WMD commission concluded that "the intelligence community fundamentally misjudged the status of Iraq's BW [biowarfare] programs" and that the "central basis" for its misguided assessment "was the reporting of a single human source, Curveball," who proved to be a fabricator. The commission observed that "the Curveball story" is one of "poor asset validation by our human collection agencies; of a tendency of analysts to believe that which fits their theories; of inadequate communication between the intelligence community and the policy makers it serves; and ultimately, of poor leadership and management."

The Curveball story is also one of high-level confrontation, between George Tenet and John McLaughlin on one side, and Tyler Drumheller, a genial and rotund man who was the chief of the European Division in the CIA's Directorate of Operations, on the other.

Drumheller tried to prevent Curveball's lies from getting into Colin Powell's UN presentation, and his experience provides a vivid glimpse into the hothouse atmosphere at CIA headquarters in the months before the invasion of Iraq.

Perhaps the most shocking thing about the American reliance on Curveball was the fact that U.S. intelligence officials never even met him before the war and couldn't talk to him directly. Curveball was an Iraqi exile who served as a source for the German intelligence service, and the Germans refused to provide the United States with direct access to the informant. The Germans claimed that Curveball would refuse to talk to the Americans, and so they would only provide reports based on their own debriefings of the Iraqi.

What was worse for the CIA, the agency wasn't even receiving the reports directly from the Germans. Instead, Berlin provided Curveball debriefing reports to a U.S. military intelligence unit, the Defense HUMINT Service, which then circulated the reports throughout the U.S. intelligence community. Defense HUMINT distributed the reports without any vetting of Curveball's information. The CIA decided it was willing to accept these thirdhand reports.

With no ability to question Curveball and almost no way to corroborate what he was saying, the U.S. intelligence community still fully embraced Curveball's assertions. The October 2002 National Intelligence Estimate on Iraq's weapons of mass destruction concluded that Iraq has "transportable facilities for producing bacterial and toxin BW agents." The NIE said it had multiple sources for that assertion, but in fact it was based almost entirely on Curveball.

But even as Curveball's reports were being given the stamp of approval in the NIE, Tyler Drumheller was beginning to hear warnings about the source—from the Germans themselves. As chief of the DO's European Division, Drumheller was in charge of the agency's liaison relationships with Western European intelligence services, and so in the fall of 2002, he had lunch with the Washington station chief of the German intelligence service. With war looming, Drumheller asked if the Germans were now willing to grant the Americans direct access to Curveball. The German station chief replied that meeting the source wasn't worthwhile, because Curveball was crazy. It would be a waste of time. The German told Drumheller that his service wasn't sure Curveball was telling the truth, and worse, that there were questions about his mental stability and reliability, particularly since he had suffered a nervous breakdown. The message was painfully clear: the Americans shouldn't use Curveball's information.

Drumheller passed on these warnings to top CIA managers, thinking that would be the end of Curveball's reporting. "I said it is going to make us look stupid if we don't validate this," Drumheller recalled.

But Drumheller hadn't reckoned on the strength of the agency's embrace of Curveball and his pro-WMD intelligence. By January 2003, Drumheller was shocked to learn that Curveball's reporting was going to be included in Colin Powell's UN presentation, scheduled for early February.

One week before Powell made his presentation, Drumheller was shown a draft of his speech. It didn't mention Curveball or the Germans, but it did include assertions about the existence of Iraqi mobile bioweapons trailers that came straight from Curveball. Drumheller wasn't a technical bioweapons expert, but he did know about intelligence operations, and he knew that the tradecraft in the Curveball case was shoddy at best. Earlier in January, the German intelligence service had sent a cable to the CIA saying that the Americans could use Curveball's reporting in Powell's presentation—but also warning that it couldn't vouch for the information. Drumheller realized that he had to move fast to get this flawed material out of Powell's presentation, and so he called McLaughlin's assistant to set up an urgent meeting with the deputy CIA director.

At the start of the meeting, McLaughlin's executive assistant told the deputy director that Drumheller had serious problems with Curveball. McLaughlin responded in a way that surprised and troubled Drumheller.

"I hope not," McLaughlin said, according to Drumheller. "This is the heart of the case." The CIA's case that Iraq had a biological weapons program rested almost entirely on Curveball. Until that moment, Drumheller had no idea that the CIA had almost nothing else.

Drumheller quickly explained to McLaughlin how shaky the case was, and how there were concerns that Curveball might be a fabricator. As Drumheller left, McLaughlin told his assistant to "try to take care of this," and Drumheller once again felt confident that he had prevented a disaster.

"I thought they were going to drop it," Drumheller recalled. "I told the Germans they were going to drop it." Just to make sure, Drumheller's European Division sent a copy of Powell's draft speech back to top CIA managers with the Curveball material scratched out.

The night before Powell's presentation, Drumheller got a phone call at home from Tenet. The CIA director was at a New York hotel with Powell, getting ready for the presentation the next day, and Tenet needed to talk to British intelligence officials one last time to get their approval to use information from one of their sources. Tenet asked Drumheller for Dearlove's phone number. At the end of their conversation, Drumheller took the opportunity to remind Tenet that Curveball was trouble. "I said to him, boss, you know there are problems with that German reporting," Drumheller recalled. "He said, 'Yeah, yeah, I know all that.' But I don't think he was really paying attention, they had been up all weekend."

The next day, Drumheller was at work at CIA headquarters when his wife called him. She was watching Powell's presentation on television and had called to tell him quickly to turn it on. To Drumheller's astonishment, he saw that Powell was making the forceful case for the existence of an Iraqi biological weapons program based on reports of mobile weapons labs.

Drumheller turned to one of his aides. Did we send them the right version of the speech, the one with Curveball's material all crossed out? Yes, they had.

A German intelligence official called. I thought you got them to take that out, the confused German said.

As late as May 2003, as doubts began to surface that there might not be any WMD in Iraq, the CIA was still trying to smother those doubts by issuing a paper stating that two trailers discovered in Iraq cinched the case that Iraq had mobile biological laboratories. In fact, analysts later acknowledged that the trailers they had discovered were used to pump hydrogen into weather balloons; the weather balloons were to be used by the Iraqis to help gauge wind conditions for its conventional artillery.

When the independent WMD commission investigated the Curveball case, it questioned both Tenet and McLaughlin, asking about Drumheller's efforts to block the use of Curveball's information. McLaughlin told the commission that he did not recall the meeting with Drumheller a week before Powell's presentation. Tenet told the commission that he remembered calling Drumheller looking for Dearlove's telephone number, but he didn't remember any warnings about Curveball. Drumheller has been deeply disappointed and angered by their answers to the commission.

"I think Tenet believed that they would find WMD when they got to Iraq and that nobody would remember these questions," said Drumheller.

"Why didn't anybody say anything before the war [about how weak the intelligence was]? I did. And I can tell you it was hard, because nobody wanted to hear it, and they made it very clear that they didn't want to hear it."

* * *

The CIA's management team pushed aggressively on Iraqi WMD intelligence despite the fact that it had known for years that the agency's intelligence on Iraq was dangerously weak. Jack Downing, who served as the CIA's deputy director of Operations from 1997 to 1999, recalls that the agency's inability to recruit spies in Iraq was a glaring weakness widely recognized by top CIA officials at the time. He said he repeatedly tried to address the problem throughout the late 1990s, but was frustrated that the agency's Near East Division, in charge of espionage in the Middle East, never came up with any workable answers.

"We kept pounding away on the issue of why don't we have any sources in Iraq?" Downing recalled. The chief of the Near East Division "would come in with these PowerPoint presentations to show that they were trying things, but none of them ever worked. I knew that it was hard to get sources, it was difficult because we didn't have any diplomatic presence in Iraq, but we still should have been able to get some. Nothing much ever worked."

Top agency officials were well aware of this failure. In the 1990s, Tenet had created a special "hard-target" committee made up of senior agency officials, which periodically reviewed the status of the CIA's intelligence collection on the highest-priority issues, such as Iraq, Iran, and North Korea. Those reviews showed clearly to top CIA officials just how blind the agency really was when it came to Iraq, according to one former participant in the agency's hard-target reviews. "Everyone [involved in the hard-target review process] knew that we didn't have any sources in Iraq," the former participant said.

In the later stages of the Clinton administration, the CIA actually removed Iraq from the hard-target priority list, according to former participants in the process. At the time, Iraq appeared to be contained by sanctions and the U.S. no-fly zones, and didn't appear to be a threat to the United States. While Iraq was being downplayed as an intelligence target, resources were shifted to focus more on Iran, several CIA sources said. That shift in resources took place in the late 1990s, and it meant that when the Bush administration came into office, the CIA's capability to spy on Iraq had been allowed to wither.

It is unclear whether these glaring gaps in the intelligence were ever clearly explained to President Bush. It is entirely possible that the doubts shared by many CIA officials about the quality of the intelligence on Iraqi WMD were kept away from the White House. If so, that self-censorship may have involved the most important document produced by the CIA—the President's Daily Brief, an exclusive report sent to the president each morning containing a summary of the day's most important intelligence. One senior former CIA official reports that frustrated CIA staffers came to him to tell him that there had been articles written for the President's Daily Brief that raised questions about the evidence concerning Iraqi WMD, but that those articles were removed from the PDB before it was sent to the White House. It has not been possible to confirm these claims with other sources. But it does not appear that the President's Daily Brief ever reflected the level of skepticism about the quality of the intelligence that was widespread within the CIA.

Of course, it is hard to say how Bush might have reacted if he had received a PDB that raised doubts about the existence of Iraq's weapons programs. He too might have ignored the warnings or even dismissed the articles. But it is also possible that he would have asked a few follow-up questions, which might then have forced the CIA to provide better supporting evidence for its many other reports that stated flatly that Iraq did have WMD programs. If someone had spoken up clearly and forcefully, the entire house of cards might have collapsed. A little bit of digging might have revealed the truth. A postwar investigation by the Senate Select Committee on Intelli-

gence suggested that hard questions could have made a difference—
most of the key judgments in the intelligence community's October
2002 National Intelligence Estimate, the Senate panel concluded,
were either "overstated, or were not supported by the underlying intelligence reporting." The independent WMD commission went
further, flatly stating that the intelligence community's prewar assessments about Iraq's weapons of mass destruction "were all
wrong."

George Tenet is certain to be remembered in history for one memo-
rable phrase: slam dunk. Ever since Bob Woodward disclosed in his
book *Plan of Attack* that Tenet had assured President Bush that the
case for the existence of Iraqi WMD was a "slam dunk," the phrase
has stuck to Tenet and has transformed him into the face of one of the
greatest intelligence failures in history.

After the war, Tenet seemed angered that the White House appeared to hold him responsible for many of the WMD intelligence
failures—at least until President Bush awarded him a Presidential
Medal of Freedom. Tenet and other top CIA officials remained defensive about the CIA's failures on prewar intelligence long after the
U.S. invasion of Iraq.

In early 2004, David Kay, the CIA's chief WMD hunter in Iraq,
broke with the agency and said publicly that there were no weapons.
Kay had one final, private meeting with Tenet during which Kay realized the degree to which Tenet had become personally invested in
the existence of Iraqi WMD. Kay believed that the CIA director was
still in denial about the deeply flawed nature of the prewar intelligence and seemed to be looking for some thread to hang on to.

As Kay was about to leave, he recalled that Tenet said: "I don't
care what you say. You will never convince me they didn't have
chemical weapons."

Finally, in 2005, Tenet admitted publicly that the "slam dunk" quote was accurate and ruefully acknowledged that those were the two stupidest words he had ever uttered.

By the time American troops were ready to invade Iraq in March 2003, it was too late for anyone to consider the truth. The Iraqi regime desperately sent out a series of back-channel messages to try to tell the Americans that there were no illicit weapons, but no one was willing to listen.

One of the most bizarre efforts by Baghdad to open a back channel with Washington came through an unlikely source, a Lebanese-American businessman named Imad Hage. A Maronite Christian, Hage had lived for years in the United States before returning to Beirut, and had developed important contacts in Washington, including Richard Perle, the influential neoconservative and outside advisor to the Pentagon. Hage had also made intriguing contacts in Lebanon, including with a leading Syrian figure, who, in the weeks before the invasion of Iraq, put Hage together with Iraqi intelligence officials eager to get a message to Washington.

Hage agreed to fly to Baghdad, where he met with the chief of the Iraqi intelligence service. He told Hage that Iraq had no WMD, and to prove it the regime was willing to let the Americans in to look for themselves. Hage then flew to London to meet with Perle, and told him the Iraqis wanted to meet him to talk.

Perle called a senior CIA official to see whether there was any interest. The CIA official told Perle that the only message they had for the Iraqis was that "we will see them in Baghdad," Perle later recalled.

And so the war came. The initial invasion was a swift triumph, a masterful exhibition of America's conventional military power. The invasion went more smoothly than many imagined because Iraq didn't use any chemical, biological, or nuclear weapons against U.S. troops. The protective gear American soldiers carried across the Kuwait-Iraq border turned out to be just excess baggage.

Baghdad fell with little resistance, and before long, the CIA was ready to reopen its Baghdad station for the first time in more than a decade.

6

SPINNING WAR AND PEACE

T HE POST-INVASION period in Iraq proved to be far more difficult than anyone had hoped. Unfortunately, the Bush administration and the CIA were still so deeply politicized that the truth took a long time to sink in.

The Third Armored Cavalry Regiment of the United States Army has a long and proud history, a tradition dating back to the Indian wars of the American West. First organized in the 1840s as the Regiment of Mounted Riflemen, it was renamed the Third United States Cavalry in the Civil War, the Third Cavalry Group Mechanized in World War Two, and finally the Third Armored. The regiment was born as a frontier unit, forged in the heat and dust of Texas, and it has been fighting native insurgencies in remote and godforsaken places since the days of Geronimo.

By fall 2003, the Third Armored Cavalry, now equipped with Apache attack helicopters and Bradley fighting vehicles rather than horses and carbines, was in western Iraq, trying to seal the porous Syrian border and prevent foreign jihadists from flooding in from around the Arab world. The regiment's First Squadron was guarding the key border town of al Qa'im, about 200 miles northwest of

Baghdad, and had settled into Tiger Forward Operating Base in an old train station on the outskirts of al Qa'im.

In early November, the CIA's Baghdad station chief came to Tiger FOB as part of a tour of outlying U.S. military units in order to get a better feel for conditions around the increasingly restive country.

In the al Qa'im train station that day, a young commander said something foreboding to the CIA station chief that brought clarity out of the noise and confusion of the looting and violence that had marked the early months of the American occupation of Iraq. The army officer looked at the CIA station chief and said, matter-of-factly: "The war is about to begin."

The officer explained that over the last four to six weeks, something new had been happening in his area of responsibility. The Iraqi insurgents were coalescing, exhibiting in their tactics and methods greater command, control, and sophistication. The insurgents were getting better—and more deadly. It was obvious to the officer that the rebels were gearing up for something bigger, and that the Third Armored Cavalry, and the rest of the American Army, was on the verge of a new war for Iraq.

The officer's observations confirmed what the CIA station chief had begun to piece together himself from intelligence reports and his travels around Iraq. There had been intermittent attacks on American and international targets and a steady, but still modest, stream of casualties since U.S. troops entered Baghdad in April. Now the violence was evolving into something much worse. The relative quiet and broad popular support that the Americans had enjoyed in the first days of the occupation following the ouster of Saddam Hussein had proven to be a false dawn. Now, the U.S. military was starting to face a well-armed guerrilla force with nearly unlimited resources, and the rebels were dedicated to throwing the Americans and their provisional government out of Iraq. The U.S. commanders in the field, like those with the Third Armored Cavalry, could sense it. It was coming at a faster pace every day, and it gave the CIA station chief a very bad feeling.

The station chief returned to Baghdad convinced that he had to issue a report to CIA headquarters offering a broad reassessment of conditions in Iraq. He had already written one assessment of the situation in August, but now things were getting much worse. The United States, he believed, was in danger of losing a war that it thought it had already won.

That November the CIA station chief wrote a painfully honest account of the worsening situation. It pulled no punches in detailing how the new insurgency was gaining strength from the political and economic vacuum that the United States had allowed to develop in Baghdad. He wrote his report in the form of an "aardwolf," a nickname for a CIA station chief's formal assessment of conditions in his country. (The nickname came from an oddly striped type of African hyena and had stuck through generations of CIA officers.)

There was only one problem: He had committed the unpardonable sin of telling the truth.

The station chief's unvarnished warning of looming trouble in Iraq was a shot across the bow for the Bush administration. It couldn't go unanswered. He soon found himself facing piercing questions from CIA officials stemming from a series of inflammatory accusations about his personal behavior, all of which he flatly denied. Worse, in early 2004 the station chief began to sense that he was about to be turned into a scapegoat for the CIA's involvement in prisoner abuse at Abu Ghraib prison. He decided to quit the CIA in disgust. Later, he would trace his troubles back to his decision to write the unsparing truth about the growing insurgency and the failures of American policy to address the underlying problems that were fueling the war in Iraq.

Former top CIA officials familiar with the matter deny that the

station chief was removed from his post because of his critical aardwolf report. They say instead that the Baghdad station had grown so
large that the job had become too much for the young officer to handle. The station had a staff of seventy to eighty people in midsummer
2003, but that figure surged to more than three hundred by the end of
2003, and later grew further still, making it by far the largest CIA
station in the world, and the largest since the agency's Saigon station
at the height of the Vietnam War. There was so much going on, the
former officials add, that the young station chief made serious mistakes, including his failure to monitor closely CIA interrogations at
Abu Ghraib prison. The station chief was replaced with a more senior and more experienced officer.

While those problems certainly did exist, it is also true that the
station chief was not the only CIA officer to encounter career troubles after expressing skepticism about Iraq. In fact, while the pressures on the CIA from the Bush administration concerning the
handling of prewar intelligence have been well documented, it is
now clear that such pressures continued long after the invasion. It became evident to officers in the field that intelligence reports raising
questions about the conduct of the war and the problems being en-
countered in Baghdad because of the Bush administration's policies—or lack of policies—were not welcome in Washington.

The sudden downfall experienced by the station chief following
his candid report in November 2003 convinced other CIA officers
that there was a steep price to be paid for writing unvarnished intelligence reports about Iraq. "When I read that November aardwolf,"
said a CIA official who knew the Baghdad station chief, "I thought
that he was committing career suicide."

Certainly, CIA officers stationed in Iraq learned to tread carefully. Sources say, for example, that they tried to avoid writing intelligence reports about Ahmed Chalabi, the former Iraqi exile who
had close ties to the Pentagon's leadership. Reporting on Chalabi
would only cause trouble. Many U.S. officials in Baghdad came to

suspect that ragtag, armed groups affiliated with Chalabi's camp were involved in looting and thievery in the chaos following the toppling of Saddam Hussein—but nothing was done about it, and no one wanted to report what they saw back to Washington. When Chalabi's supporters raced to seize many of the files of Saddam Hussein's Baath Party and the former regime's intelligence service, neither the U.S. military nor the CIA intervened. CIA officials later said they suspected that Chalabi used the files against his political enemies. But CIA sources say that Chalabi's direct connection to Deputy Defense Secretary Paul Wolfowitz and other top Pentagon officials made him virtually untouchable.

Chalabi remained in good standing with the Pentagon until the spring of 2004 when he was accused of revealing to Tehran that the United States had broken the communications codes of the Iranian intelligence service and that the Americans were reading Tehran's secret communications. (Chalabi steadfastly denied any wrongdoing, maintaining that the charges were a CIA smear.)

This did lead to a break in relations with Chalabi but only for a time. One of the greatest political survivors of modern times, Chalabi would later reinvent himself once more by aligning with radical Shiites like rogue cleric Moqtada al-Sadr, in order to gain popular support in Iraq. In April 2005 he would be named one of two deputy prime ministers and interim oil minister. In November he would be meeting in Washington with top administration officials, including Rice, Rumsfeld, and Cheney.

As the insurgency worsened and the Bush administration fumbled for answers, the consequences to those who provided honest intelligence reporting became more obvious. In 2004, case officers stationed in Baghdad told their colleagues that they were frequently ordered to revise intelligence reports that were considered "negative" about Iraq. And in late 2004, when a new CIA station chief—the successor to the officer pulled in December 2003—wrote another aardwolf reporting on the deadly conditions in Iraq, his political allegiances were quickly questioned by the White House, CIA officials later learned. After his aardwolf circulated in Washington, then–U.S. Ambassador John Negroponte heard from an official at the National Security Council. The NSC wanted to know whether the CIA officer was a Republican or a Democrat.

The pressures extended even down to the level of CIA officers involved in the interrogation of captured Iraqi officials. According to CIA sources, most of the high-level members of Saddam Hussein's former regime who were captured by U.S. forces after the invasion provided little useful information. But one who did was Abid Hamid Mahmud al-Tikriti, the presidential secretary to Saddam Hussein and dubbed the "Ace of Diamonds" in the U.S. military's famous deck of cards identifying the highest-ranking members of the Iraqi regime. As one of Saddam's closest confidants, he had been in charge of Saddam's personal security and had controlled access to the Iraqi president. He was one of the few people who knew the innermost secrets of the bloody history of the Iraqi regime.

After he was captured in June 2003, the CIA assigned one of its best Arabic speakers, a woman who fully understood the nuances of the language, to question the presidential secretary. But what the Iraqi told his interrogator did not fit with what Washington wanted to hear. He said, for instance, that Saddam Hussein had not been at Dora Farms, a compound outside Baghdad, when the United States launched a bombing raid against the site at the start of the war in an attempt to kill the Iraqi leader and quickly decapitate the regime.

Saying that Saddam was not at Dora Farms was inconvenient for Washington on several levels. A year before the war, the CIA had virtually no spies with inside knowledge of Saddam Hussein's regime. But just before the war, the agency's Iraq Operations Group suddenly recruited an entire network of agents. This overnight network was dubbed the ROCKSTARS. They were paid huge sums of money in return for what they claimed was insider information. The ROCKSTARS might have seemed too good to be true, but for the CIA, which had not had any decent spies inside Iraq in years, the ROCKSTARS were too tempting to pass up.

Just two days before the American invasion was scheduled to be launched, a ROCKSTARS agent reported that there was unusual activity at a compound known as Dora Farms, outside Baghdad, and that it appeared that Saddam Hussein, and possibly his two ruthless sons, were staying there. CIA Director George Tenet rushed the information to the White House, and the president quickly ordered a strike by cruise missiles and Stealth aircraft against the site in an attempt to kill Saddam and perhaps shorten the looming war.

Saddam was not killed in the strike, but the CIA and the Bush administration invested heavily in the notion that the attack had nearly killed the Iraqi leader. For the CIA, and Tenet in particular, it would be difficult to acknowledge that the information had been wrong. (In an interview, a former Iraq Operations Group officer said that the ROCKSTARS provided valuable intelligence and stressed that Saddam was at Dora Farms.)

Another awkward disclosure came when the presidential secretary said that Saddam fled Baghdad by driving through a U.S. military checkpoint without being recognized. In addition, Abid Hamid Mahmud al-Tikriti told his interrogator that Iraq had no weapons of mass destruction, that the WMD had all been long since destroyed. When he said this, in June 2003, the United States was still conducting its postwar hunt for the banned weapons, and finding them was an important political objective for the Bush administration. Before the war, the CIA had concluded that Mahmud al-Tikriti was one of the only top officials of the Iraqi regime who had release authority over the country's WMD, so he was believed to be one of the few who knew where they were hidden. What did it mean that he was telling his interrogator that there were no such weapons?

CIA headquarters decided that Mahmud al-Tikriti was lying,

and that his female CIA interrogator was not pressing him enough. She had developed "clientitis" and was going too easy on the Iraqi, CIA headquarters complained. She was too accepting of his lies. CIA officials ordered that she be replaced.

It was part of a pattern. "The people who were running things and the people who were getting promoted were politically responsive" to the administration, said one CIA source.

Still, the biggest problem facing U.S. intelligence officers in postinvasion Iraq was the same thing that plagued the U.S. military—the glaring fact that no one had developed a plan for what to do after American troops got to Baghdad. The White House had, strangely, left the job of postwar planning up to the Pentagon, cutting out the State Department, which had been studying the issue for a year and had put together detailed plans for reconstruction. But the Pentagon leadership had no serious interest in postwar planning. They equated it with "nation building," a term that had been discredited in the 1990s among conservatives, who associated it with Clinton administration foreign policy. President Bush had campaigned against nation building during the 2000 presidential race, and Pentagon hard-liners still opposed it, even while the United States was invading and occupying two countries in two years. They argued that the U.S. military should fight and not dissipate its resources in rebuilding after combat.

The White House had to know the consequences of the Pentagon's reticence about reconstruction well before the Iraq War, since Rumsfeld and other Defense officials had earlier resisted such involvement in Afghanistan. After the quick military victory over the Taliban in the fall and winter of 2001, President Bush pledged in early 2002 that the United States would not allow Afghanistan to fall back into chaos. But inside the Bush administration, Rumsfeld and the Defense Department were initially reluctant to take responsibility for building a new Afghan Army, which was needed to give back-bone to the fragile new government in Kabul, according to former administration officials.

When it came to Iraq, the Pentagon believed that it had the silver bullet it needed to avoid messy nation building—a provisional government in exile, built around Chalabi, could be established and then brought in to Baghdad after the invasion. The exiles could step in and take over, in a kind of turnkey operation.

But President Bush vetoed that idea, repeatedly telling his top advisors that he did not want the new government of Iraq to be chosen in Washington. It had to be chosen by the Iraqi people. Several officials say that Bush personally made it clear just before the invasion that the United States would not set up Chalabi as the new leader of Iraq.

Bush's commitment to democracy was laudable, but it was not really an answer to the question of postwar planning. Once Bush quashed the Pentagon's plans, the administration failed to develop any acceptable alternative. To be sure, the NSC staff led an interagency team that came up with policy guidelines to be used during the postwar period. The team's conclusions were briefed to President Bush and his senior advisors just before the invasion and included recommendations to keep the regular Iraqi Army largely intact and to keep de-Baathification of the Iraqi government to a minimum. Both of those recommendations were ignored. Instead, once the Pentagon realized the president wasn't going to let them install Chalabi, the Pentagon leadership did virtually nothing. After Chalabi, there was no Plan B. "Part of the reason the planning for post-Saddam Iraq was so nonexistent was that the State Department had been saying if you invade, you have to plan for the postwar," recalled one former official in the Bush White House. "And DOD said, no you don't. You can set up a provisional government in exile around Chalabi," and then the U.S. military could swiftly pull out. "DOD had a stupid plan, but they had a plan. But if you don't do that plan, and you don't make the Pentagon work with State to develop something else, then you go to war with no plan."

Administration officials still argue that there was a plan for what they called "Phase IV," or the postinvasion stage of Operation Iraqi Freedom. The plan called for the creation of an organization called the Office of Reconstruction and Humanitarian Assistance (ORHA), to be run by retired Army Lt. Gen. Jay Garner, who had been in charge of providing assistance to Kurdish refugees following the first Gulf War in 1991. But the Bush administration saw ORHA's mission as temporary, one designed to feed and house refugees and turn the lights on in Baghdad and help get the Iraqi infrastructure up and running, until new Iraqi leadership emerged. No one figured out before the war how they were going to get from ORHA to a new Iraqi leadership. ORHA was soon replaced by a cumbersome new organization called the Coalition Provisional Authority, run by Paul Bremer, a former State Department official. The Pentagon continued to oversee the occupation, and the CPA reported directly to the Defense Department. Soon, Republican operatives and conservative ideologues flooded into Baghdad to work for the CPA. They sought to turn Iraq into a laboratory for conservative ideas that they had not yet been able to sell in the United States. But while they were fiddling with their pet projects, Baghdad was starting to burn.

Officials at the White House and Pentagon convinced themselves that the lack of planning was in reality a visionary approach. In a highly revealing postinvasion interview with *The Atlantic* magazine, Undersecretary of Defense Doug Feith proudly acknowledged as much. "You will not find a single piece of paper," Feith told *The Atlantic*. ". . . If anybody ever went through all of our records—and someday some people will, presumably—nobody will find a single piece of paper that says, 'Mr. Secretary or Mr. President, let us tell you what postwar Iraq is going to look like, and here is what we need plans for.' If you tried that, you would get thrown out of Rumsfeld's office so fast—if you ever went in there and said, 'Let me tell you what something's going to look like in the future,' you wouldn't get to your next sentence!"

The damaging effects of the lack of any serious planning might have been reduced if the U.S. military had gone into Iraq with many more troops—with enough force to lock down the entire country and prevent chaos until some kind of new government emerged. But Rumsfeld strongly opposed recommendations for more force from army leaders who believed the invasion was being planned with a dangerously small force. When Army Chief of Staff Gen. Eric Shinseki told Congress in February 2003, just weeks before the invasion, that several hundred thousand troops would be needed in postwar Iraq, both Rumsfeld and Wolfowitz publicly attacked him, since they had both been arguing that the war could be won with a much smaller force. The idea that the war might be a painful drain on the military was heresy. Shinseki was pushed aside. The message was not lost on other American military commanders: don't complain about the resources available for the war in Iraq if you want to keep your job. Bush and Rumsfeld would later both claim that they were always prepared to send more troops to Iraq if commanders in the field requested them. But the generals had learned not to ask.

At first most Iraqis did welcome the Americans as liberators, just as Pentagon conservatives had predicted. As a result, the Bush administration was granted a brief grace period in which it still could have moved to bring stability to the country. Instead, the Pentagon and the CPA, encouraged by Chalabi, launched a damaging purge of Baath Party members from key government positions in Iraq, and then compounded that action by quickly demobilizing the Iraqi Army.

Membership in Saddam's Baath Party had been crucial to personal advancement in the old government, so de-Baathification removed most of the people who had been responsible for making the Iraqi government work. Disbanding the Iraqi Army, meanwhile, sent hundreds of thousands of soldiers home without paychecks, converting them into natural recruits for a rebellion.

Combined, the two actions convinced the Sunni elite, a minority that had been ruling Iraq for centuries, that the Americans were determined to overturn its traditional hold on power. The Bush administration was not going to stop at ousting Saddam Hussein; it was going to topple the existing class structure of Iraq. American policies were having the effect of ripping power away from the Sunni Muslims and handing it to Iraq's long-suffering Shiite majority, which was certain to come out on top in direct elections. This was social engineering on a historic scale, akin to Reconstruction in the post–Civil War American South. When Iraq's embittered Sunnis turned against the occupation, the United States had no effective response. The insurgency began to grow.

The Bush administration initially dismissed the new insurgency as scattered acts of terrorism that did not represent a serious threat. Car bombings and guerrilla activity were said to be desperate acts of "dead-enders" who would wilt away once Saddam Hussein was captured. In fact, the insurgency was made up of a complex mix of forces, and it was sometimes difficult to determine whether they were working together or along parallel tracks. There were some foreign jihadists and al Qaeda sympathizers, most notably the ruthless group led by Abu Musab al-Zarqawi, a Jordanian-born terrorist. It was a sad irony that these jihadists were turning Iraq into a terrorist haven *after* the American invasion, not before it.

Yet the number of foreign Arab fighters was small. The insurgency was dominated by former intelligence officers and other members of Saddam Hussein's regime. The CIA later determined that they had planned for guerrilla war before the U.S. invasion by setting up secret weapons caches and stay-behind networks. The CIA eventually discovered, for instance, that just before the war, Iraqi intelligence agents had purchased large numbers of garage door openers in Dubai, as crude but effective remote triggering devices for roadside bombs.

The Baathists relied heavily on foot soldiers and sympathy drawn from the disaffected Iraqi Sunni community, and without popular support in the so-called Sunni Triangle of Iraq, the insurgency could not have been sustained. In late 2003, Bremer and the CPA finally recognized they had to reach out to the Sunnis, and launched a so-called Sunni initiative to try to connect with Sunni leaders who might be willing to cooperate with the Americans. But by that time, Sunni leaders or other political figures who openly worked with the CPA were seen as collaborators and faced the threat of assassination by the insurgents.

Within the Bush administration, no one wanted to suggest that the insurgency was at least in part a nationalistic rebellion fueled by Sunni anger and resentment. That would give it too much political credibility. The Pentagon was prepared to violate the cardinal rule of warfare—know thine enemy. It is no wonder that reports suggesting that conditions in Iraq were deteriorating were greeted in Washington as if they were partisan political attacks.

Like the Pentagon, the CIA also failed to plan ahead. On the eve of battle, the CIA had little information to offer U.S. military commanders about what kind of political climate they could expect to find when they finally got to Baghdad. In the months before the invasion was launched, Lt. Gen. David D. McKiernan, the commander of all land forces for the invasion, made an ominous admission to a senior CIA officer. He said that he was concerned about what was supposed to happen when the army got to Baghdad; he didn't know who the military was supposed to link up with once Saddam's regime was gone. The general wanted to know who was going to serve as the intermediary between the U.S. military and the Iraqis to make sure that things kept running in the country. Unfortunately, the CIA officer had to admit that the agency didn't have any answers. It didn't have any sources or agents in Baghdad who could help the Americans coordinate with local Iraqi leaders to keep the government running. In fact, no one at the CIA had even done any serious thinking about the problem.

Instead of addressing pragmatic issues like those troubling General McKiernan, the CIA focused before the invasion on covert action programs, including expensive plans for the war that were never implemented. With a dash of bravado and a sense of hope, the CIA created a secret Iraqi paramilitary force and nicknamed it the Scorpions. Training under the watchful eyes of U.S. Special Forces and CIA instructors at an isolated military base in the Jordanian desert, the Scorpions learned the black arts of covert action, deception, and sabotage. In late 2002 and early 2003, the CIA invested millions of dollars in the Scorpions to get them ready for a historic assignment: to start a war.

In many ways, the Scorpions, made up of Iraqi exiles, were the CIA's covert answer to the Pentagon's Free Iraqi Forces, a group of Iraqi exiles with ties to Chalabi who had been trained in Hungary before the invasion. But in contrast to the Pentagon, the CIA took great pains to make certain that it kept Chalabi's influence out of the Scorpions, screening out those with ties to Chalabi and his organization.

The CIA's plans for the Scorpions were ambitious, rooted in the agency's desire to play a leading role in the initial stages of the Iraq invasion. The CIA hoped to use the Scorpions at the outset of the war to conduct acts of sabotage inside Iraq, as well as for largely symbolic acts that could sow confusion within Saddam Hussein's regime. One proposed plan called for the Scorpions to be flown by helicopter across the border at the outset of the war and then dropped near an Iraqi military base. Dressed as Iraqi soldiers, they would stage a mutiny, to make it seem as if the Iraqi Army were beginning to rebel against Saddam Hussein. That action could also convince others in the Iraqi Army to defect and join in the liberation of their country.

The CIA's Directorate of Operations spent vast resources on the Scorpions, despite skepticism among some in the CIA about the effectiveness of the operation. One CIA source described the group as a paramilitary "fantasy" that had no chance to have a significant impact on the course of the war. Ultimately, plans to use the Scorpions in the opening phase of the war were canceled, despite the investment, because of opposition from senior U.S. military commanders who believed the CIA-trained teams would only get in the way.

Without the Scorpions, the CIA's main role inside Iraq during the initial stages of the invasion came through joint teams set up with U.S. Special Forces to provide tactical intelligence support to the main invasion force as it moved toward Baghdad. These teams tried to develop local contacts in cities near the main invasion routes in order to scout out the opposition and potential points of resistance. Some of these teams did provide valuable information to the conventional military, particularly in southern Iraq.

But thanks to weak planning and management controls at the agency, these teams were vulnerable to being misused, according to CIA sources. In fact, as the invasion progressed through southern Iraq, a case officer assigned to one of the special teams found himself wrestling with an order he believed was completely out of bounds, one that seemed to have echoes of Vietnam.

According to a CIA source, while the young case officer was traveling with one of the teams, he received a call from another CIA official. The CIA officer told the young case officer to assign one of his Iraqi agents to eliminate a local Iraqi whom the agency believed was a problem. It was clear to the young case officer that the official was trying to get him to order the killing of the local Iraqi. In effect, the CIA official was trying to use the joint CIA–Special Forces team as an assassination squad.

"That shows you the mentality of the people running this thing," said the CIA source.

Instead, the case officer contacted a senior CIA officer and told the senior officer about the order. The senior officer told him not to obey the order and not to order the killing. The young officer obeyed, and the killing did not take place. Yet the order for the killing of a local Iraqi has apparently never been investigated by the CIA, according to the agency source.

In the days immediately after the fall of Baghdad in April, the CIA continued to conduct operations in Iraq without adequate planning or foresight, sometimes with tragic results. Eager to encourage the emergence of pro-American Muslim leaders in Iraq, the CIA arranged in early April 2003 for a moderate Shiite cleric, Abd al-Majid al-Kho'i, to fly into Iraq from his exile in London. The cleric was not a CIA asset, but the agency believed he could be a stabilizing influence in the Shiite community. The decision to fly him into Iraq was made over the objections of CIA officers in the field, who warned that conditions in the country were still too dangerous.

But the warnings were ignored, and on April 10, 2003, al-Kho'i was murdered in Najaf almost as soon as he had returned to Iraq. American officials suspected that radical Shiite cleric Moqtada al-Sadr was behind the murder, in order to eliminate a potential rival for clerical leadership.

Some U.S. intelligence officials recognized before the invasion that the U.S. occupation of Iraq would present opportunities for new kinds of intelligence collection inside Iraq. In practice, however, many of those opportunities were squandered because of the lack of planning for the postinvasion period. American sources say, for example, that the National Security Agency had a plan to create a front company that would have managed cellular telephone service in postwar Iraq. That would have given the NSA the ability to eavesdrop on every cell phone call in the country and would have made it extremely difficult for insurgents to use electronic communications without being detected by American intelligence. But sources say that the NSA delayed its plans for so long that the CPA under Paul Bremer finally opened cell-phone franchises to bidding by private companies.

The CIA station chief who wrote the November 2003 aardwolf that sparked so much controversy was actually the agency's second chief in postwar Baghdad. He took over in July 2003. A senior CIA officer had served as the first Baghdad station chief immediately after the invasion, but he only stayed in Iraq briefly, just long enough to get the CIA station up and running. Conditions were eroding so rapidly that by August, the second CIA station chief was already convinced that he needed to issue his first aardwolf to warn Washington. The August report, written one day after a deadly bombing of the United Nation's offices in Baghdad that killed the UN's top official in the country, was so grim that it immediately caused a stir within the CIA and the Bush administration, and even prompted a tart rebuttal from Bremer.

The August aardwolf said that the UN bombing was part of a strategy by a new and bold insurgency to discredit and isolate the U.S.-led coalition, and warned that insurgents and terrorists had the capability to carry many more attacks against "soft targets." The insurgency was increasingly dangerous and threatened to erase the early progress made by the Americans and could actually overwhelm occupation forces. It accurately identified two strands of violence— coming from foreign mujahideen and Iraqi insurgents—and stated ominously that there was "no shortage" of combatants. It also predicted that the capture of Saddam Hussein was unlikely to end the insurgency, since he did not seem to be leading it.

Coming so soon after the euphoria in Washington over the toppling of Saddam, the August aardwolf seemed to many within the

Bush administration to be far too negative. Bremer was so concerned by the tone of the aardwolf that he felt compelled to write an accompanying note at the end of the report, in which he downplayed its analysis of the worsening conditions in Iraq. He said it overestimated the threat posed by the insurgency, and he added that he did not think it was clear that this "low-intensity conflict" could erase American gains in Iraq, even if the rebellion grew worse. On balance, he said, reconstruction in Iraq was going forward despite the insurgency.

As the violence continued to worsen in the summer and fall of 2003, there was increasing tension within the Bush administration over the best ways to respond. A major issue was how best to focus intelligence resources to help identify and capture or kill insurgents.

The problem was that the CIA was stretched thin. For political reasons, the White House wanted the CIA to conduct the hunt for Saddam Hussein's weapons of mass destruction. The Pentagon's initial WMD-hunting efforts had been so amateurish that President Bush had personally asked CIA director George Tenet to take over the task. Tenet had asked former UN weapons inspector David Kay to lead a new team, the Iraq Survey Group, to scour the countryside looking for any evidence of chemical, biological, or nuclear weapons.

By the fall, Kay's team had hit a series of dry holes. Meanwhile, the insurgency was worsening, and so the CIA station in Baghdad began pushing for a shift of intelligence resources away from the hunt for WMD and toward efforts to counter the insurgency. U.S. military commanders were also pushing for a redeployment of the Iraq Survey Group to counterinsurgency work.

Tenet agreed to redeploy some of the Iraq Survey Group, but he still pushed for the CIA's Baghdad station to keep hunting for WMD, and that led to tensions between Baghdad and CIA headquarters. CIA officers in Baghdad thought that headquarters was forcing them to continue a wild goose chase.

In January 2004, just as David Kay went public with his belief that there was no WMD in Iraq, a CIA manager gave the staff of the Baghdad station an unusual deadline. Tenet was being forced to testify before Congress about the hunt for WMD, and the director had to explain to lawmakers why nothing had been found. David Kay was making life uncomfortable for Tenet, and he didn't want to have to walk into the hearing room empty-handed. So the CIA manager at headquarters told the Baghdad station staff to launch a new, last-gasp effort to find some weapons of mass destruction. "The director is on the Hill in seven days, let's refocus on finding the WMD," the official said. Unfortunately, Baghdad station could not find any weapons to appease Tenet.

The tension between the political demands for WMD and the more pressing need to fight an increasingly deadly insurgency was one of several underlying themes behind a series of constant battles between the Baghdad station and CIA headquarters over resources and manpower in the first year after the invasion.

One of the most pressing problems was a shortage of CIA officers in the Baghdad station who could speak Arabic. The CIA was flooding Iraq with officers on temporary assignment, drawn from all over the world, but few had experience in the Arab world, and even fewer could speak Arabic. Many were rookie officers on their first overseas tour of duty. By the fall of 2003, the station had just four case officers who could speak the language, making it extremely difficult for many of the officers in the station to conduct clandestine operations effectively in the country.

There was also a shortage of analysts who could improve the agency's understanding of the insurgency. CIA analysts sitting back in Langley couldn't get a feel for the rapidly changing nature of the rebellion, and the Baghdad station began pushing CIA headquarters to send analysts to Iraq who could help make sense of the reports coming in from the field. Finally, by the end of 2003, the CIA had about thirty intelligence analysts deployed to Baghdad. More than nine months after the invasion, they began to unlock elusive clues from the intelligence that allowed them to begin to map the structure of the insurgency.

Ever since the summer of 2003, the Baghdad station had realized that one of the biggest mistakes being made in Iraq was the failure to conduct a systematic effort to obtain intelligence from Iraqi insurgents who had been captured. The U.S. military was doing a poor job of identifying and questioning important detainees; it didn't even know how many foreign fighters it was holding among the thousands of detainees in its prisons. The CIA agreed to take on the job of interrogating the most important detainees to gather intelligence on the insurgency. But CIA headquarters refused to give the Baghdad station the resources or the legal guidelines it needed to do the job effectively and within the limits of U.S. law.

The Baghdad station's leaders repeatedly asked Langley to provide its case offices with training in interrogation methods, to make certain that they were conducting the sessions with the prisoners in the proper manner. But CIA headquarters failed to provide the training. As early as July 2003, the station asked CIA headquarters for written guidelines on how to conduct detainee interrogations. CIA headquarters wouldn't provide them, leading to heated arguments. After months of frustrating delays, tensions erupted during one secure videoconference call between Baghdad and Langley when the deputy station chief in Baghdad started yelling at headquarters staffers, demanding that they provide the written guidelines for interrogations that the station had requested. The only response came from the Near East Division chief, who told the Baghdad station chief that his deputy was becoming "too strident" on the issue. The guidelines were never delivered before the Abu Ghraib prison abuse scandal erupted.

CIA headquarters also initially failed to provide Baghdad with a lawyer to handle legal questions related to the conduct of prisoner interrogations. Instead, the station had to search for legal advice on an informal basis, from other CIA or military lawyers who happened to be passing through Baghdad. The agency didn't send a lawyer to Baghdad to deal with the legal aspects of detainee interrogations until January 2004, and then only after the army had begun its internal investigation of prisoner abuse at Abu Ghraib.

For the Baghdad station, the most sensitive issue related to detainee interrogations involved "ghost detainees"—prisoners who were not immediately registered in military prisons while they were questioned by the CIA. Another controversial practice involved the movement of some ghost detainees out of Iraq. During 2003, there were six to eight people captured in Iraq who were taken by the CIA to be interrogated in other countries, including Jordan, Saudi Arabia, and Afghanistan.

Sources say that "ghosting," including the practice of transporting some prisoners to other nations, was approved by senior CIA officials, and only later did they order that the detainees be quietly shipped back to Iraq, when they realized that the practice could be in violation of the Geneva Conventions. (According to a report in the *Washington Post,* the Justice Department went so far as to draft a memo authorizing the CIA to move detainees out of Iraq for interrogation.)

While CIA headquarters was deaf to requests from the Baghdad station for more help with interrogations, no one in Washington ignored the station chief's grim second aardwolf in November, entitled "The Expanding Insurgency in Iraq." Its political implications were hard to miss.

As of early November 2003, the aardwolf explained, the insurgency in central and northern Iraq was gaining momentum and beginning to tip the balance against the Americans. The insurgents were "self-confident and believe they will ultimately succeed in returning to power as they have in the past." The rebels could sense that American political will was "wavering" and felt very little pressure from American military operations. They were more agile than the U.S. military, the report warned, while politically, they were taking advantage of the fact that the United States had not developed a clear message that was resonating with the Iraqi people.

As a result, Iraqis realized that the Baathists were still powerful, despite the ouster of Saddam Hussein. In the Sunni heartland, the Baathists appeared "largely unchallenged." Yet at the same time, the Iraqis perceived political drift in Baghdad.

The Americans, the report suggested, had blown their best chance to stabilize Iraq. The Iraqi regime had been surprised by the speed with which the Americans won the war, the report said, and so the Baathists had been off balance in the immediate aftermath of the fall of Baghdad, and they had melted away into the Sunni heartland.

But it was now clear, the report said, that the regime had not been decisively defeated, but rather only dispersed. And the failure of the Americans to establish a firm grip on the country gave them an opportunity to make a comeback. "By the end of the summer, the continued sense of isolation in the Sunni heartland, the complete dissolution of the army and other institutions of security, rigid de-Baathification, and the lack of economic opportunities or political direction gave these regime elements the confidence they needed to repair their networks and reestablish themselves. The ease with which the insurgents move and exist in Baghdad and the Sunni heartland is bolstering their self-confidence further."

Top CIA officials initially praised the November aardwolf, and one told the Baghdad station chief that it was the best aardwolf he had ever read. The aardwolf clearly caught the attention of the White House and Pentagon. In early December, the station chief was asked to brief President Bush.

But, as noted, the high-level attention was a double-edged sword, and the station chief was now completely off message. Senior U.S. military officers in Baghdad bitterly complained that they had been "blindsided" by the aardwolf, and tensions grew between the CIA and the Pentagon. Just days after the station chief briefed Bush, he was told that he would not be going back to Baghdad.

By 2005, the CIA station chief's November 2003 aardwolf would seem prescient. After the chief was pulled out of Baghdad, the insurgency only got worse, and American casualties soared. Iraq's Sunni population still felt alienated from the new political process, which was dominated by the Shiites and Kurds. Iraq became a magnet for foreign jihadists, providing a new breeding ground for al Qaeda. Islamic extremists—primarily Sunnis—who came to Iraq to fight the Americans were becoming battle hardened.

"Today, Iraq is the Super Bowl for jihadists," said one American intelligence official. The connection between Iraq and al Qaeda was finally complete.

7

LOSING AFGHANISTAN

B Y NOVEMBER 2004, Colin Powell was a lion in winter, a sad yet still regal figure who seemed to personify an era of great Republican statesmanship that was passing away. As he quietly slipped out of office in the aftermath of George W. Bush's reelection, a fitting epitaph for his tenure as Secretary of State was, perhaps, that he was a giant of a man who deserved better.

Four years earlier, he had joined the Bush administration with great promise, a genuine American hero whose credibility with the nation easily outweighed that of the inexperienced new president. The former general had campaigned for Bush during the 2000 presidential race, and Bush had made it clear to voters that if he were elected, he would appoint Powell to be his Secretary of State and would make him the leader of his foreign policy team. Powell's presence by Bush's side was a reassuring sight for voters, and it encouraged many to believe that Bush would adhere to the same centrist, pragmatic approach to foreign policy that had been the hallmark of his father's time in the Oval Office. With Powell at State and Dick Cheney—his father's Secretary of Defense and one of Powell's old partners in Desert Storm—as his running mate, George W. Bush seemed to be signaling to the public in 2000 that if you vote for me, you will get the second coming of the successful team that forged an international coalition to liberate Kuwait and also brought a peaceful end to the Cold War.

That was certainly what Powell had expected, but he also thought there was more. He returned to public service with the ambition of following in the footsteps of another who had made the transition from wartime general to diplomat, George C. Marshall, Harry Truman's Secretary of State and the architect of the Marshall Plan.

One of Powell's great strengths—and perhaps his fatal flaw—was his deep sense of loyalty, a trait ingrained during his career in the military and polished into a political attribute through his years in top jobs in the Reagan and first Bush administrations. It was not difficult for him to extend his close association with President George Herbert Walker Bush, whom he served as chairman of the Joint Chiefs of Staff during the Persian Gulf War, to Bush's son.

But over time, Powell's sense of loyalty became a heavy burden. None of the high expectations for Powell were realized; he became a marginalized figure, trapped in an administration over which he had little influence. To the surprise of almost everyone in Washington—and perhaps to Powell himself—he was repeatedly outmaneuvered on foreign policy by Secretary of Defense Donald Rumsfeld and by Cheney, who returned to government from his years in business with a far less flexible mind-set than many of his old colleagues could remember from his days in the first Bush administration. Cheney's transformation, in particular, seemed to mystify Powell.

Throughout his constant battles with Rumsfeld's Pentagon, his surprising break with Cheney, and his obvious misgivings about the invasion of Iraq, Powell's sense of loyalty demanded that he stay, at least through one full term. He seemed content to play a civilizing role, to try to mediate between the ascendant conservatives in Washington and the rest of the world.

Powell developed a few moderate allies, including CIA Director George Tenet, but ironically it was his trust in Tenet that ultimately led to Powell's greatest disaster. With Tenet's assurances, Powell agreed to go to the United Nations to make the administration's case against Saddam Hussein in February 2003, and Powell put the full weight of his name and stature behind what turned out to be deeply flawed intelligence on Iraq's supposed weapons of mass destruction. His reputation never completely recovered. (In the aftermath of Hurricane Katrina in the fall of 2005, when the competency and credibility of the Bush administration was once again under question, Powell told ABC News that he recognized that his flawed UN presentation on Iraqi WMD had tarnished his reputation, although he insisted that he did not blame Tenet personally for providing him with inaccurate intelligence.)

After America's initial triumph in Baghdad turned into bloody stalemate, Powell's loyalty to Bush came to seem more like bureaucratic passivity. Criticism mounted, and by the end, his dream of joining George C. Marshall in the pantheon of great American statesmen seemed more distant than ever.

Both Powell's good intentions and his political weakness in the face of Rumsfeld's skillfull infighting were on display in one of the last meetings of the Bush war cabinet that he attended, not long after Bush's reelection. Fittingly, on the agenda for the November 2004 meeting was the place where it all began for the Bush team—Afghanistan.

At the time, the Bush administration was trying its best to ignore the harsh realities of Afghanistan. The White House had not yet faced up to the unintended consequences of George W. Bush's most fateful decision as president—to invade Iraq before the job against al Qaeda was finished. And so now, not only was Osama bin Laden still on the loose somewhere along Pakistan's lawless frontier, but Afghanistan, threatened by an unprecedented surge in opium production, was dangerously close to becoming a narco-state.

In public, President Bush and his senior advisors continued to hail Afghanistan as an unalloyed success, and there certainly were reasons for optimism. Afghanistan was a country where Islamic extremists and global terrorists had been routed by an American-led coalition in favor of a new democratic government and a more tolerant way of life. Turnout for the Afghan elections in October 2004 was high, despite the threat of violence, and the electoral triumph solidified the position of Afghan President Hamid Karzai, a U.S. client who had returned to Afghanistan from exile in Pakistan in 2001 escorted by a phalanx of CIA officers and U.S. Special Forces troops.

At a time when conditions in Iraq were worsening by the day, the last thing the Bush administration wanted to do was tarnish the image of success in Central Asia. But deep in the bowels of the State Department, in its counter-narcotics policy shop, the Bureau for International Narcotics and Law Enforcement Affairs (INL), there was a darkening sense of doom about Afghanistan. Assistant Secretary of State Bobby Charles, who ran INL, was watching the new numbers rolling in from the Central Intelligence Agency on the unchecked growth in opium production in the Afghan countryside with a sense of disbelief.

A protégé of House Speaker Dennis Hastert, Charles was, at heart, a creature of the Republican Congress, not of the Bush White House, and he had a keen sense of how issues played with Republican lawmakers on Capitol Hill. He knew that drug trafficking was always a hot-button issue. If the American people became broadly aware of the scale of the drug crisis in Afghanistan—and that the United States was not doing anything about it—he realized that congressional sentiment would quickly shift.

Every time the CIA issued a new classified estimate on the size of the Afghan poppy crop, the numbers worsened, and Charles felt compelled to tell anyone in the administration who would listen that Washington had to do something. It wouldn't be long, he warned, before political progress in Afghanistan was drowned under a flood of opium. "I started clanging the fire bell," he recalled. "You had to take it seriously or it would devour the democracy."

Charles had Powell's solid support, but he was deeply frustrated that his warnings were being tuned out at the White House, and that his fears—both about the Afghan drug crisis and its potential political consequences—were not widely shared within the administration. In early 2004, he heard veiled and indirect complaints from the White House about downbeat testimony he gave to Congress on the problem, and yet Charles couldn't mask his own growing pessimism. He was so concerned that he soon was being called "Cassandra" around his own office, while a White House official warned him that he was becoming "inconvenient" because he refused to remain silent on Afghanistan's worsening conditions. When he persisted in late 2004, Charles was told that he was now "highly inconvenient."

Eventually, Charles would be forced out of his job by new Secretary of State Condoleezza Rice in early 2005.

Senior Bush administration officials had displayed a complete lack of interest in the Afghan opium problem ever since 9/11. In fact, the White House and Pentagon went out of their way to avoid taking on the Afghan drug lords from the very outset of U.S. military operations in Afghanistan against al Qaeda and the Taliban in the fall and winter of 2001.

According to a CIA source, after the 1998 bombings of two U.S. embassies in East Africa by al Qaeda, the U.S. intelligence community created an interagency team to identify potential bombing targets in Afghanistan to be used in any military operations against the terrorist network's Afghan sanctuary. That targeting team kept working even after President Clinton ordered a halfhearted cruise missile strike on al Qaeda terrorist camps just days after the East Africa bombings. By 2001, the team had generated a comprehensive list of potential bombing targets throughout Afghanistan.

The list included twenty to twenty-five major drug labs, warehouses, and other drug-related facilities. After the September 11 attacks, the interagency team turned its list of potential targets over to the U.S. military, but the Pentagon and White House refused to order the bombings of any of the drug-related facilities on the list, according to the CIA source. "On the day after 9/11, that target list was ready to go, and the military and the NSC threw it out the window," said the CIA source. "We had tracked these [targets] for years. The drug targets were big places, almost like small towns that did nothing but produce heroin. The British were screaming for us to bomb those targets, because most of the heroin in Britain comes from Afghanistan. But they refused." If the United States had bombed those facilities, the CIA source added, "it would have slowed down drug production in Afghanistan for a year or more."

The decision not to bomb the drug labs in the weeks after 9/11 was the first sign that the White House and Pentagon wanted nothing to do with "nation building" problems like narcotics in Afghanistan. American troops were there to fight terrorists, not suppress the poppy crop, and Pentagon officials didn't see a connection between the two. The Pentagon feared that counter-narcotics operations would force the military to turn on the very same warlords who were aiding the United States against the Taliban, and that would lead to another round of violent attacks on American troops. According to one former NSC official, Undersecretary of Defense Doug Feith argued in a White House meeting in February 2002 that counter-narcotics was not part of the war on terrorism, and so Defense wanted no part of it in Afghanistan. "We couldn't get Defense to do counter-narcotics in Afghanistan," recalled the former NSC official.

What's more, President Bush's decision to invade Iraq meant that there were severe limits on the numbers of U.S. troops available for deployment to Afghanistan. Even if the Pentagon had been ordered to do more about the drug trade, it didn't have enough troops on the ground to do the job effectively.

Once the Taliban had been routed, top CIA officials had little interest in the drug problem, either. Even as some CIA officials were urging the bombing of Afghan drug labs after 9/11, the agency's senior management was gutting the staffing of the agency's counternarcotics center in order to meet the demands of counterterrorism.

The counter-narcotics job in Afghanistan was initially left up to the British, who cared deeply about the issue since so much Afghan heroin ended up on London's streets. (Only more recently has the United States become a growth market for Afghan heroin, now accounting for as much as 10 percent of the traffic.) Yet Britain had far fewer military and intelligence resources available in Afghanistan than did the United States, and so 2002—the first year that Afghanistan was effectively under American control—saw a dramatic revival of the opium trade.

Opium production had been cut at the end of the Taliban's rule, although not for altruistic motives. In 2001, the Taliban officially banned the cultivation of opium, yet the U.S. Drug Enforcement Administration later reported that it believed the ban was imposed in an effort to raise prices on Taliban-controlled heroin in the face of a glutted market. (The Taliban had large stockpiles of opium in warehouses at the time of the U.S.-led invasion of Afghanistan, according to former U.S. officials.) Still, the Taliban cutbacks meant that Afghan opium production in 2001 bottomed out at just 74 metric tons.

Once the new American-backed government took control in Kabul, opium production skyrocketed. With controls from the central government effectively lifted, Afghanistan's production capacity for oven-dried opium soared to 1,278 metric tons in 2002, according to DEA statistics. Production more than doubled in 2003, and then nearly doubled again in the next year, and by 2004, Afghanistan was producing 87 percent of the world's opium supply. In late 2004, the CIA estimated that 206,000 hectares were under poppy cultivation, and that the new crop would generate $7 billion worth of heroin. "There is no other country in the world that has 206,000 hectares under cultivation of any drug," observes Charles.

Heroin was Afghanistan's leading export and the engine driving the country's economy. With the Americans in charge, the drug business was booming; there were reports of sixty-truck convoys loaded down with opium crossing the border from Afghanistan into Iran. Afghanistan was on the verge of surpassing Colombia as the illicit-drug capital of the world.

Inevitably, the new, U.S.-backed Afghan government was becoming badly corrupted by the heroin trade. Even as President Bush was hailing Afghanistan as an unalloyed success story, the "narco-state" label was beginning to stick.

By 2005, the United States suspected that at least one senior official in the Afghan government was corrupted by the drug trade, according to American officials, while Afghanistan's regional governments were in even worse shape, particularly in the Afghan provinces where the poppy crop was flourishing the most. American sources say that some regional officials in Afghanistan now make huge sums of money by taxing drug traffickers for their opium and heroin shipments, rather than seizing them.

With money from the booming opium trade coursing through Afghanistan, there are growing suspicions that many of the same Afghans who have received large amounts of money or other forms of support from the United States government since 9/11 are now either involved in the Afghan opium business or have been corrupted by money stemming from drug smuggling.

For years, unproven conspiracy theories about the CIA's role in cocaine trafficking from Latin America have abounded. Now in Afghanistan, the heroin trade is so pervasive that there are certain to be serious questions raised in the future about whether the CIA, the

U.S. military, and the rest of the Bush administration got too close to Afghans enmeshed in the global heroin business. Barnett Rubin, one of America's leading experts on Afghanistan, wrote in 2004 that Rumsfeld has met with Afghan military commanders "whom Afghans know as the godfathers of drug trafficking. The message has been clear: help fight the Taliban and no one will interfere with your trafficking."

The policies quietly put in place by the Defense Department—and particularly the rules of engagement for U.S. troops—certainly didn't help allay such suspicions. The Pentagon's rules of engagement for U.S. forces in Afghanistan said that if U.S. troops discovered drug shipments or drug supplies, they "could" destroy them; that was very different from issuing firm rules stating that U.S. forces *must* destroy any drugs discovered. The permissive guidance for American troops was a sign that countering drugs was not a priority, and meant that there would be times when American commanders on the ground would have the option of allowing drug shipments to pass unimpeded, particularly if the drugs were under the protection of an Afghan warlord whom the United States did not want to antagonize.

By 2003, there were reports that American troops were ignoring shipments of opium when they discovered the drugs during searches in Afghanistan. Mark Schneider, senior vice president of the nonprofit International Crisis Group, said that during a trip to Afghanistan in November 2003, he was told by U.S. military commanders and State Department officials that they were frustrated by the rules of engagement. A Green Beret who served in Afghanistan and who has since left the military said that, in private, U.S. commanders on the ground were much more blunt. He said he was specifically ordered to ignore heroin and opium when he and his unit discovered them on patrol.

Drug trafficking was taking place virtually right in front of the American military. "In some cases they were destroying drugs, but in others they weren't," complains Charles. "Rumsfeld didn't want drugs to become a core mission."

Even more troubling than the ambiguous guidelines was the fact that the United States had intelligence on the locations of key heroin processing laboratories and warehouses, particularly in southeastern Afghanistan, and yet was doing nothing to interrupt their operations. This new intelligence came on the heels of the earlier targeting information that had been ignored during the initial invasion of Afghanistan. Once again, the Pentagon refused to order that the labs and warehouses be bombed, even though Charles and other American officials were certain that the destruction of the labs and supply facilities would have had a significant impact on the Afghan opium business.

The case for targeting the infrastructure as the choke point in the Afghan drug trade was underlined in January 2004, when a British special forces team operating in Afghanistan called in an air strike on a drug lab by a U.S. Air Force A-10 aircraft. The resulting damage led quickly to a 15 percent spike in heroin prices. (It is unclear whether senior American commanders knew at the time that the proposed target in the bombing raid was a drug lab, but it was not followed up with further bombing raids on drug facilities.)

"We had regular reports of where the labs were," notes Charles. "There were not large numbers of them. We could have destroyed all the labs and warehouses in the three primary provinces involved in drug trafficking—Helmand, Nangarhar, and Kandahar—in a week. I told flag officers, you have to see this is eating you alive, that if you don't do anything by 2006 you are going to need a lot more troops in Afghanistan."

To emphasize his point, Charles asked the CIA to analyze where the drug money was going in Afghanistan. The answer was chilling. The agency told Charles that it was probable that some of the drug

profits were being funneled into the Islamic Movement of Uzbek-
istan, an al Qaeda–related group; the Hezb-i-Islami Group, controlled by an anti-American renegade, Gulbuddin Hekmatyar; the
Taliban; and possibly al Qaeda itself. The connections between drug
trafficking and terrorism that the Pentagon didn't want to acknowledge were real and growing, and were clearly helping to fuel a revival of guerrilla activity in Afghanistan. "The linkages were there,"
argues Charles.

Throughout 2004, Charles's concerns were shunted aside by the Pentagon and the White House, but he persisted, and by the end of the
year he and his staff at the State Department were still pushing for a
comprehensive Afghan counter-narcotics program. In effect,
Charles wanted the United States to transplant to Central Asia many
of the counter-narcotics tactics it had applied with some limited success in Latin America.

The most controversial of his proposals was an aggressive plan
for the aerial spraying of the Afghan poppy fields, something that the
Pentagon opposed for fear that it would incite anti-American violence. Charles knew that there was strong opposition among
Afghans to aerial spraying; false rumors that the United States was
secretly spraying crops in rural Afghanistan had triggered protests
and rampant conspiracy theories in the countryside. But Charles believed that Washington could gain support in Afghanistan—as it
had in Colombia—if it launched a serious public campaign in support of spraying while providing significant aid for alternative agri-
cultural development. The spraying could be conducted with the
herbicide glyphosate, which is used by many Americans on their own
gardens under the trade name Roundup. He was prepared to take a
team of scientists to Kabul to show the Karzai government that a
highly diluted version of glyphosate could be safely and effectively
sprayed from the air with no serious health risks. He also tried to

arrange a conference with five hundred leading Afghan mullahs to convince them to support a public campaign outlining the dangers of heroin and to gain support for spraying.

But U.S. Ambassador Zalmay Khalilzad, along with Rumsfeld and Deputy Defense Secretary Paul Wolfowitz, shared his opposition to an aggressive counter-narcotics program and repeatedly blocked Charles's efforts in Kabul. Charles eventually became convinced that Karzai voiced objections to stronger counter-narcotics measures only because he was under pressure from Rumsfeld and Khalilzad to resist the State Department's efforts.

In addition to an aerial spraying campaign, Charles kept pushing for a more aggressive drug interdiction campaign—but that meant that the Defense Department had to change its guidance to American commanders in Afghanistan. The Pentagon had to tell the U.S. Central Command, which was in charge of military operations in Afghanistan, to start conducting missions to destroy drug labs and storage and production hubs.

The bureaucratic forces of the Pentagon were still arrayed against Charles when Powell came to the White House for the post-election meeting of the war cabinet to gain the president's endorsement of the State Department's counter-drug initiative. With Bobby Charles riding the back benches in the cramped White House Situation Room, Powell was prepared to fight one of his last battles inside the Bush administration.

Colin Powell was nothing if not a great briefer, and President Bush seemed to be listening intently as Powell smoothly laid out the facts behind the growing drug problem and the State Department's proposals to counter the threat. Bush appeared to be taken by the issue, and he seemed genuinely troubled that the heroin trade had become such a major problem. Bush made supportive comments as Powell made the case for aerial eradication while emphasizing that the military had to be given new rules of engagement. Powell underlined the need for action by telling the president that it was crucial that the United States not lose its hard-won gains in Afghanistan.

Not only did Bush say that he agreed with Powell, but he force-fully added that he was determined not to "waste another American life on a narco-state," stressing that the United States had to destroy the poppy crop.

Charles was dumbfounded and silently elated as he listened to Bush; he was nearly floored by Bush's use of the "narco-state" term, something Bush would not have uttered in public. It proved to Charles that the president understood the stakes. It appeared to Charles that he had suddenly won his prolonged bureaucratic battle with the Pentagon; after all, the president of the United States had just spoken and had emphatically endorsed a war on Afghan opium.

But Charles was soon to learn to his bitter disappointment that the president of the United States did not always have the last word in the Bush administration. Charles was about to discover what Colin Powell already knew: Donald Rumsfeld and his lieutenants treated the president's statements as nothing more than the start of negotiations.

Time and again in the Bush administration, Rumsfeld simply ignored decisions made by the president in front of his war cabinet, according to several senior administration officials. Condi Rice, who was supposed to be managing the interagency policy process, seemed either unwilling or unable to rein in Rumsfeld, so the defense secretary simply got away with pursuing his own foreign policy.

Rumsfeld succeeded by using a passive-aggressive style in which he would raise an unending series of questions and concerns about a proposal without flatly stating his opposition to it. If a decision went against him in one meeting, he and his aides would simply arrange another meeting with a different group of administration officials and would repeat the process until the Pentagon view prevailed. Rumsfeld succeeded by wearing out his bureaucratic foes, and by refusing to take no for an answer, even from the president. That separated Rumsfeld from Powell, who made the mistake of playing by the rules.

Within weeks of the November 2004 war cabinet meeting in which the president had so enthusiastically endorsed the State Department's counter-drug plan for Afghanistan, Charles learned that the plan was, in fact, dead.

During the war cabinet meeting, Rumsfeld, who participated through a secure videoconference link, had repeatedly interjected with objections. When that didn't seem to dissuade the president, Rumsfeld and his allies continued the debate through back channels after the meeting was finished. In December 2004, as Colin Powell prepared to leave the government and the State Department was effectively leaderless, the Rumsfeld camp struck back. Charles was told that Khalilzad arranged for a private meeting with Bush, during which he told the president that as ambassador, he needed flexibility in how he dealt with the drug problem. Bush agreed, saying he just wanted the job done. Left unsaid was the fact that giving Khalilzad flexibility meant that almost nothing would get done.

Bush did not push back against the Rumsfeld-led opposition. The aggressive campaign of aerial spraying was abandoned in favor of a token "ground eradication" effort, which meant sending a group of Afghans in to pull up a few hundred acres' worth of poppy plants by hand. Almost none of the crop was destroyed. By mid-2005, the U.S. military finally began conducting some raids against drug-related targets, but the new interdiction effort seemed to have little impact on the heroin trade. For Afghanistan's drug lords, business was very good under the United States Central Command.

Flush with drug money, the insurgency in Afghanistan intensified in the summer of 2005 to its most dangerous levels since the American invasion nearly four years earlier. There were steady reports that the rebels, a confusing mix of Taliban, al Qaeda, and others, were surprisingly well armed and equipped—evidence that they were also well financed. The Bush administration had purchased an illusion of stability in Afghanistan at the price of billions of dollars' worth of heroin that was flooding into the streets of Europe and the United States.

The Bush administration's lack of interest in fighting the Afghan heroin business was painfully evident in its secret handling of one of the strangest cases of the post-9/11 era: the pursuit and capture of Haji Bashir Noorzai, the top Afghan drug lord of the Taliban era.

In the 1990s, Haji Bashir Noorzai watched as the peasant-led, Pakistani-sponsored Taliban movement gained power in Afghanistan. Where others saw the fearful rise of Islamic extremism, he saw dollar signs. Noorzai, a member of a large and extended Afghan clan, developed a close alliance with Mullah Omar, the young Taliban leader and Islamic fundamentalist. Through Omar, Noorzai gained a dominating position in the Afghan opium trade. Noorzai also developed close ties to al Qaeda and Pakistani intelligence, and before long he was playing a dangerous yet highly lucrative role at the intersection between the Taliban and the outside world.

This arrangement worked extraordinarily well for Noorzai—until 9/11. When the American-led invasion of Afghanistan forced the Taliban from power, Noorzai lost his primary patron.

As the Taliban faced defeat in late 2001, American sources say that Mullah Omar entrusted Noorzai with as much as $20 million in Taliban money for safekeeping while Omar and other Taliban leaders melted away. Then Noorzai took a giant risk, surrendering to the U.S. military in Afghanistan. Sources say he was detained and interrogated in late 2001. But Afghanistan's most powerful drug kingpin was released by the Americans after a few days of questioning.

After his release, Noorzai was spooked when one of his business partners was killed in an American raid, and so he disappeared. It now appears that he moved freely throughout Pakistan, where he had set up drug-processing laboratories, and that he had little trouble traveling around the Middle East. American sources say that it was later discovered that he had been given a passport by Pakistani intelligence officers.

Noorzai adapted to the post-Taliban world and developed connections with some influential figures in the new Afghanistan, including at least a few who also had close ties to the U.S. government, according to sources familiar with Noorzai's case. But Noorzai never stopped looking over his shoulder and was clearly fearful that the United States would eventually come looking for him. And so in 2004, Noorzai agreed to hold secret talks to discuss a deal with the Americans.

U.S. sources say that a special team, working on behalf of the FBI, arranged to meet with him, first in Peshawar, Pakistan. The message the Americans delivered to Noorzai was a simple one: you can keep on running, or you can come work with us. Cooperate, and tell us what you know about the Afghan drug business, al Qaeda, the Taliban, and their financiers.

Noorzai seemed willing and agreed to travel to the United Arab Emirates to try to hammer out an agreement. Noorzai was not completely trusting, however; the intermediaries who put the Americans in contact with Noorzai had to agree to have some of their relatives held as hostages by Noorzai's men. If anything happened to Noorzai during his talks with the Americans, the hostages would be killed. "This was very difficult to arrange," said one American source, with noted understatement.

But the Bush administration was so distracted by Iraq—and seemed to care so little about the Afghan drug crisis—that it couldn't be stirred to action even when an Afghan drug kingpin came in from the cold to talk. While Noorzai waited in a hotel in the United Arab Emirates with members of the covert U.S. team in the fall of 2004, an FBI delegation was supposed to fly out to join them to cut a deal. But the FBI agents never arrived, and so the talks couldn't be held, according to people familiar with the case. American sources add that the local CIA station in the UAE was so preoccupied with the war in Iraq that it was unable to devote any attention to the Noorzai case.

The operation fell apart. Noorzai cooled his heels in the United Arab Emirates, waiting in vain for the FBI, but finally began to get suspicious that he was being set up. The Americans waiting with him told him the truth—Washington was preoccupied by Iraq—and so Noorzai quietly slipped away. He still had powerful friends, including officials in Pakistan's intelligence service, so he was able to melt away once again.

"We let one of the big drug kingpins go, someone who was a key financier for al Qaeda, someone who could help us identify al Qaeda's key financiers in the Gulf," said an American familiar with the case. "It was a real missed opportunity. If the American people knew what was going on, they would go nuts."

Finally, six months later, in the spring of 2005, the special American team, this time with the backing of the Drug Enforcement Administration, found a way to get back in contact with Noorzai. Once again, he agreed to meet with them. The Americans asked Noorzai to come to the United States to negotiate a deal, and to the astonishment of nearly everyone involved in the case, he agreed. Noorzai flew on a regular commercial flight to New York, where he was met by federal agents.

The Bush administration was so startled that he had actually agreed to come to the United States that it was not quite sure what to do with him. Rather than arrest him right away, the FBI and DEA agreed to put him up in a hotel in New York for several days while they talked to him. Noorzai was in a legal netherworld, and his presence in the United States was kept secret.

Eventually, the government lost patience with the pace of its talks with Noorzai and decided to arrest him. Federal prosecutors finally held a press conference to announce his indictment in April 2005, although they refused to explain to the confused press corps how an Afghan drug kingpin had ended up in New York City.

By the summer of 2005, Noorzai was in jail and was talking, but questions remained about whether the Bush administration really wanted to hear what he had to say, particularly about the involvement of powerful Afghans and Pakistanis in the heroin trade.

As drug-fueled violence worsened and American casualties increased in Afghanistan in 2005, the tragedy was that it was still just a sideshow. Nearly four years after 9/11, American military operations in Afghanistan had more to do with maintaining the stability of the Karzai government than with fighting global terrorism. Worse, the hunt for Osama bin Laden, the original rationale for the American presence in Afghanistan, was badly stalled.

The problem was so simple that nobody was talking about it. The United States had deployed tens of thousands of troops to both Iraq and Afghanistan, but bin Laden was not in either country. Bin Laden was in Pakistan, and had been since December 2001. The most wanted man in the world was sitting safely across the border from the Americans, thinking about how best to strike the West again.

The rapid fall of Kabul and the rout of the Taliban and al Qaeda in the winter of 2001 brought a badly needed taste of victory to America just two months after the devastating September 11 attacks and seemed to signal a new way of war, one in which few U.S. conventional forces would be required.

In reality, the American operation did not go as smoothly as it appeared on television. U.S. sources say that in the weeks between the September 11 attacks and the start of the U.S. bombing campaign in Afghanistan in October 2001, U.S. intelligence located Osama bin

Laden, but the U.S. military was not prepared to strike him. Intelligence officials say that at the time, the U.S. military was developing a plan for an air campaign over Afghanistan that was not flexible enough to take advantage of the sudden windfall of intelligence concerning bin Laden. This little-known opportunity to kill bin Laden came before the terrorist leader fled into the mountains of southeastern Afghanistan, where he became much more difficult to track.

The broader Afghan campaign was also slowed by a secret debate within the Bush administration over how vigorously to support the Northern Alliance, the Afghan rebel group that had been battling the Taliban for years. The Northern Alliance was dominated by Tajiks, an ethnic minority from the Afghan north. Some American officials feared that if the Northern Alliance seized Kabul, Afghanistan's Pashtun majority in the south would respond by launching another civil war. Administration officials also feared that Pakistan, which backed the Pashtuns, would oppose a Tajik takeover in Kabul. As this policy debate dragged on in Washington, American bombers were ordered to focus their attacks on Afghan government infrastructure targets in Kabul and elsewhere, far from the battlefields in the north, and the Taliban front lines were left relatively unscathed.

According to *First In,* a recent book by Gary C. Schroen, who led the first CIA team into Afghanistan after 9/11, it was thought that if the Taliban government was weakened before its frontline troops gave way, perhaps a Pashtun force would rise up in the south, defeat the Taliban, and seize Kabul before the Northern Alliance could break through. The limited air campaign delayed the Northern Alliance's progress and gave al Qaeda leaders extra time to prepare their escape.

Once intense air raids were finally targeted directly on the Taliban frontlines, first near the key northern town of Mazar-i-Sharif, the results were spectacular, ending any further debate. The Northern Alliance quickly broke through to Kabul. The Taliban melted away. Yet bin Laden and the remnants of his organization were able to make it to the relative safety of al Qaeda's old terrorist training compounds in the mountains of southeastern Afghanistan.

In hindsight, it is now clear that December 2001 was the moment when the Bush administration's strategy in the global war on terror began to lose focus. The Taliban was on the run, and bin Laden and the hard core of al Qaeda were cornered in the White Mountains at Tora Bora, against the Pakistani border.

But the Pentagon did not deploy enough American troops to seal off the area, on either side of the border. Army Gen. Tommy Franks, the chief of U.S. Central Command and in overall charge of U.S. operations in Afghanistan, was under intense pressure from Rumsfeld to limit the number of U.S. troops being deployed to the country, according to *Not a Good Day to Die,* a recent book on the opening stages of the war by journalist Sean Naylor.

As a result, Franks lacked the conventional forces needed to corral bin Laden. Instead, the United States relied on the forces of a local Pashtun warlord, Hazrat Ali, to attack at Tora Bora. They were joined by small numbers of U.S. Special Forces and CIA paramilitary officers, backed by U.S. airpower, but the combination of elite U.S. units, airpower, and indigenous forces didn't work this time. Bin Laden escaped.

CIA officials are now convinced that Hazrat Ali's forces allowed Osama bin Laden and his key lieutenants to flee Tora Bora into Pakistan. Said a CIA source, "We realized those guys just opened the door. It wasn't a big secret." Bin Laden has been hiding on the Pakistani side of the Afghanistan Pakistan border region ever since and has never ventured out of that remote region, American intelligence officials believe.

The Bush administration has never publicly blamed Hazrat Ali for allowing bin Laden to escape, but CIA officials say there was a debate within the agency about having Hazrat Ali arrested by the new

Afghan government. That plan was abandoned and instead, Hazrat Ali emerged, under the American occupation, as the strongman of Jelalabad in eastern Afghanistan.

By early 2002, the Pakistani border province of South Waziristan was the new center of gravity for al Qaeda, but American military and intelligence forces in Afghanistan were frustrated by strict rules of engagement that prevented them from pursuing al Qaeda operatives across the border. The Pakistanis were deadly serious about keeping American forces out, and Green Berets who served in southeastern Afghanistan say that there have been a series of tense confrontations—and even firefights—between American and Pakistani forces along the border. Both sides have largely covered up the incidents.

Yet at the outset of 2002, White House officials still seemed to recognize the need to follow up on the initial success in Afghanistan with a vigorous pursuit of al Qaeda. Inside Afghanistan, they hoped to continue to apply pressure on the remnants of the Taliban and al Qaeda with the joint CIA–Special Forces units that had been so successful in supporting the rebel Northern Alliance in the rout of the Taliban in the fall and winter of 2001. It was considered crucial that these teams be in place in the spring of 2002, when the weather would improve and the traditional Afghan fighting season would begin.

Closely linked with this strategy was an innovative idea to help the CIA get at al Qaeda inside Pakistan. The CIA planned to spend $80 million to establish a new Afghan intelligence service as part of the new Afghan government; it would be a spy service staffed by Afghans but would in reality be a wholly owned subsidiary of the CIA. Having a local intelligence service based in Kabul, one that would be taking orders from the Americans, would represent an invaluable platform for targeting al Qaeda, both inside Afghanistan as well as in neighboring Pakistan. It would be easier for Afghan intelligence operatives to slip quietly across the border into Pakistan and blend into villages to gather information about al Qaeda operatives hiding out in Pakistan than it would be for American officers to do so.

But these plans were disrupted when the Bush administration shifted its focus to Iraq in the early spring of 2002 and bin Laden was given a badly needed respite. Funding for the new Afghan intelligence service was repeatedly delayed, while Special Forces teams were redeployed so they could get ready for Iraq.

Al Qaeda was back on its heels in early 2002. Senior al Qaeda operatives who were later captured said bin Laden was surprised by the ferocity of the American counterattack after 9/11. But at the moment when al Qaeda was most vulnerable, the United States relented, and the core of al Qaeda survived. The United States captured or killed more than two-thirds of the operatives who had been running al Qaeda at the time of the attacks on New York and Washington, but failed to put it out of business.

While the Bush administration turned its attention to Iraq, "discussions about Afghanistan were constrained," said one former senior NSC official. "Here's what you have now, you don't get anything more. No additional missions, no additional forces, no additional dollars." The former NSC official added that "the meetings to discuss Afghanistan at the time were best described by a comment Doug Feith made in one meeting, when he said we won the war, other people need to be responsible for Afghanistan now. What he meant was that nation building or postconflict stability operations ought to be taken care of by other governments. . . . To raise Afghanistan was to talk about what we were leaving undone."

In December 2002, President Bush met with his senior advisors to review the status of the war on terror. One participant in the cabinet-level meeting recalled that several senior officials, including Tenet, Rice, and Wolfowitz, voiced concerns about the ability of al Qaeda–style terrorists to recruit and gain support on a widespread basis in the Islamic world. Did the United States have a strategy to counter the growth potential of Islamic extremism? "The president dismissed them, saying that victory in Iraq would take care of that. After he said that, people just kind of sat down," the participant recalled.

By 2003, the Bush administration finally began to recognize that it could no longer ignore the fact that bin Laden was still on the loose, if for no other reason than he was becoming an awkward political issue in the president's reelection campaign. Late in 2003, the CIA established a series of covert bases inside Pakistan to hunt for him, with the secret approval of Pakistan's government. But the Pakistani military and intelligence service placed strict limits on the ability of the CIA officers manning the agency's secret bases to operate freely in Pakistani territory. CIA officers were forced to travel in the rugged border area with Pakistani security escorts and under the close supervision of Pakistani officials, making it virtually impossible for the Americans to conduct effective intelligence-gathering operations among the local tribes on Pakistan's northwest frontier.

By that time, al Qaeda had evolved into something more dangerous than the pre-9/11 organization; it had become a global brand name, the Nike of Islamic terrorism. Inspired by bin Laden but not always led by him, a new generation of Islamic extremists in Europe, Asia, and the Middle East were calling themselves al Qaeda. Without its state-sponsored sanctuary in Afghanistan, al Qaeda became more decentralized, like a fast-food chain with a series of regional franchises that acted in al Qaeda's name but without taking commands directly from bin Laden.

This new, horizontally structured al Qaeda lacks sophistication but is deadly nonetheless. Bloody attacks in Madrid in 2004 and London in 2005 revealed the face of post-9/11 terrorism—small local cells conducting simple, moderate-sized attacks on easily accessible civilian targets.

In a sense, this new pattern represents a triumph for American-led counterterrorist efforts. Al Qaeda now seems to lack the power to conduct another 9/11, although bin Laden still yearns to launch another "spectacular." Al Qaeda has been forced to resort to more conventional forms of terrorism—car bombs and small explosives left on buses and trains.

The great question dominating George W. Bush's second term in office is the role of the war in Iraq in the broader war against al Qaeda–style terrorism. That broader war is a multifront guerrilla conflict in Iraq, Afghanistan, and elsewhere.

Many of the fighters facing American soldiers around the world are Saudis, and are likely to return to Saudi Arabia—the birthplace of al Qaeda. There, they can continue to wage their holy war in a country that is only slowly waking up to the danger posed by al Qaeda's virulent strain of Islamic extremism.

8

IN DENIAL:
OIL, TERRORISM, AND
SAUDI ARABIA

THE FBI HAS AN evocative phrase that it uses to describe the personal effects seized from a suspect during an arrest—"pocket litter." If a criminal—or a terrorist—is carrying something on him at the time of his capture—pocket litter—chances are it has some significance. A wallet, driver's license, passport, airline tickets, personal notes, photographs, and computer discs, all contain important clues to the suspect's past activities and future plans.

The pocket litter found on Abu Zubaydah when he was captured in Pakistan in March 2002 was particularly revealing—perhaps too revealing. Zubaydah, the first high-ranking al Qaeda leader to be captured after the September 11 attacks, was carrying two bank cards, similar to American debit or ATM cards, one from a bank in Kuwait and another from one in Saudi Arabia. The discovery of the bank cards revealed that Abu Zubaydah, a top lieutenant of Osama bin Laden, had access to Western-style accounts in major financial institutions in the Persian Gulf and almost certainly had the accounts at the time of 9/11. This was an extremely rare find. An American source involved in Zubaydah's capture said he believes Zubaydah is the only top al Qaeda leader ever captured with such clear physical evidence that he was using Western-style bank accounts. Top al Qaeda leaders have instead tended to fund their activities through the use of informal Muslim financial institutions, known as *hawalas,* which have extremely loose record keeping and don't leave behind the kind of paper trail that come with banks and other Western financial institutions.

The discovery of Abu Zubaydah's cards provided some of the most tantalizing physical evidence ever uncovered related to al Qaeda. The cards had the potential to help investigators understand the financial structure behind al Qaeda, and perhaps even the 9/11 plot itself. The cards were rare finds in the field of terrorist financing investigations, one that almost never yields clear and conclusive evidence.

Tracking the murky money trail left behind by terrorists has been a frustrating and often fruitless exercise for the forensic financial sleuths at the FBI, CIA, and Treasury Department. Investigators usually have to rely on arcane "link analysis" and other circumstantial and indirect evidence to try to draw connections from among the many rivers of money coursing through Islamic charities and other nongovernmental organizations that might lead them to terrorist leaders and their plots.

As a result, American experts have often gone down the wrong path as they have tried to follow terrorist money. The CIA and FBI believed for years, for instance, that bin Laden, the son of Saudi Arabia's richest construction magnate, was funding al Qaeda's activities with his own personal wealth; they didn't understand the significance of the donations al Qaeda was receiving from other wealthy Arabs, particularly from Saudi Arabia and other Gulf states, who shared bin Laden's Islamic extremism. It took years for the U.S. government to develop a more nuanced understanding of al Qaeda and its money. Eventually, the CIA realized that bin Laden was not as wealthy as originally believed. He was a member of an enormous extended family (he was one of fifty-seven children of Mohammed bin Laden) and so Osama received a relatively small inheritance from his father's huge Saudi construction empire. In 2000, the United States determined that, instead of the $300 million he was thought to be worth, bin Laden had received only about $1 million a year from his family from 1970 until 1994. In the early 1990s, under pressure from the Saudi government, the bin Laden family had been forced to sell Osama bin Laden's share of the family construction empire, and the Saudi government later froze the proceeds of the sale. Bin Laden was simply not rich enough to fund a jihad by himself.

The CIA estimated that it took about $30 million a year to run al Qaeda's operations before 9/11, and that virtually all of the money was coming from donations—often funneled through Islamic charities and corporate fronts. Yet while American investigators developed strong suspicions about specific Islamic charities and their donors, it was always difficult for the CIA and FBI to prove which ones actually were in league with al Qaeda.

With the bank cards discovered with Abu Zubaydah, there was little need for link analysis or circumstantial guesswork. Although the cards were not in Zubaydah's name, they were clearly being used by one of Osama bin Laden's top lieutenants. An examination of the transactions in the accounts might help track the movements of the al Qaeda leadership in the crucial days before and after 9/11, while also providing a conclusive trail back to their financial backers in the Middle East. The cards had the potential to be keys that could unlock some of al Qaeda's darkest secrets. The cards "could give us entrée right into who was funding al Qaeda, no link analysis needed," said one American source. "You could track money right from the financiers to a top al Qaeda figure."

But something very odd happened when the FBI and CIA team

on the ground in Pakistan swept up Abu Zubaydah's personal belongings and bundled them back to the United States for examination. There is little evidence that an aggressive investigation of the cards was ever conducted.

Two American sources familiar with the matter say that they don't believe the government's experts on terrorism financing have ever thoroughly probed the transactions in Abu Zubaydah's accounts or vigorously pursued the origins of the funds. It is not clear whether an investigation of the cards simply fell through the cracks, or whether they were ignored because no one wanted to know the answers about connections between al Qaeda and important figures in the Middle East—particularly in Saudi Arabia.

The two American sources who have followed this remarkable story are willing to give Washington the benefit of the doubt and believe the failure to pursue the leads was a simple oversight, rather than a political cover-up to protect the Saudis. "The cards were sent back to Washington and were never fully exploited," said one American familiar with the matter. "I think nobody ever looked at them because of incompetence." There is no evidence that Abu Zubaydah has ever been questioned about the cards.

Despite the lack of interest or attention in Washington, some American investigators continued to pursue the case as best they could, on their own. But they found it difficult to get information about where the cards had been used or any other information about them, especially from Saudi officials.

Eventually, American investigators in the field recruited a source whom they believed could help solve the mystery. A Muslim financier with a questionable past, and with connections to the Afghan Taliban, al Qaeda, and Saudi intelligence, agreed to work with the Americans to try to find out what he could. In 2004, he reported that his Saudi sources had told him a stunning story. Eighteen months earlier, he said he had been told, Saudi intelligence officials had seized all of the records related to the card from the Saudi financial institution in question; the records then disappeared. There was no longer any way to trace the money that had gone into the account. The timing of the reported seizure of the records by Saudi intelligence closely coincided with the timing of Abu Zubaydah's capture in Pakistan in March 2002.

Ever since the September 11 attacks, the trail back from al Qaeda to Saudi Arabia has been an intriguing path, but one that very few American investigators have been willing or able to follow. America's energy dependence on Saudi Arabia, and the money and power that flows from Saudi oil, means that Saudi influence in American politics is pervasive. It is an issue only slightly less sensitive to discuss in polite company in Washington than that of Israeli political influence. So many people in Washington's power circles— lawyers, and lobbyists, defense contractors, former members of Congress and former White House aides, diplomats and intelligence officers, and even some journalists—rely so heavily on Saudi money or Saudi access that ugly truths about Saudi links to Islamic extremism have been routinely ignored or suppressed. In addition, Saudi Arabia's support for the war in Iraq, coupled with its intermittent efforts to try to stabilize oil prices, has been highly valuable to the Bush administration.

The Saudi investment in political power in Washington paid off in the days and weeks after the September 11 attacks. During that frantic time, when the Bush administration's counterterrorism policies were still being formulated and American public opinion about 9/11 and the roots of terror was still highly malleable, no one in Washington worked harder to earn their keep than the spin merchants of Saudi Arabia.

They were faced with a public relations nightmare of historic proportions: fifteen of the nineteen hijackers who had just killed thousands of Americans were from Saudi Arabia. They had been sent on their suicide mission by the son of one of Saudi Arabia's wealthiest and most powerful families. What was worse, the attacks on the World Trade Center and the Pentagon were winning praise from Islamist clerics and other radicals back home in Saudi Arabia, where Osama bin Laden had become a folk hero.

But despite those awkward PR issues, the Saudis successfully managed the crisis and ultimately convinced most Americans that there was an important distinction between the actions of Saudi extremists and the policies of the Saudi government and royal family.

Later, when it was revealed that members of the bin Laden family and other prominent Saudi citizens were allowed to leave the United States on special flights arranged by the Saudi government and facilitated by the FBI in the immediate aftermath of the September 11 attacks, the controversy was again muted. The independent 9/11 commission downplayed the incident, concluding in its final report that it had found "no evidence of political intervention" in the United States government to approve the flights, and that the FBI had conducted a "satisfactory screening of Saudi nationals who left the United States on charter flights" after 9/11. Yet FBI documents released in 2005 contradicted the 9/11 commission report and revealed that the FBI had not been certain whether some Saudis who left the country on the special flights had had information relevant to the 9/11 investigation.

Certainly, the power and influence over American foreign policy held by Saudi Arabia can be overstated. Critics often fall prey to dark conspiracy theories. It is easy to exaggerate the degree of Saudi complicity in the rise of al Qaeda or the 9/11 plot.

The truth is less sinister but no less dangerous. Like the leaders of other Arab states, officials in Saudi Arabia turned a blind eye to Islamic terrorism for decades, hoping that they could buy off the terrorists and appease the religious extremists who backed them while still maintaining the status quo in the region. Turning a blind eye to terrorism is very different from acting as a state sponsor of it, and since May 2003, when al Qaeda first launched a wave of terrorist attacks inside Saudi Arabia, the Saudi security services have become far more cooperative with the CIA and FBI in cracking down on al Qaeda networks operating on Saudi soil. After the Riyadh bombings in that month, CIA Director George Tenet traveled to Saudi Arabia to meet with top Saudi officials and found that the attitude about al Qaeda had completely changed. The Saudis finally recognized that al Qaeda was their enemy, too.

Yet it is still true that, both before and after 9/11, President Bush and his administration have displayed a remarkable lack of interest in aggressively examining the connections between Osama bin Laden, al Qaeda, and the Saudi power elite. Even as the Bush administration spent enormous time and energy trying in vain to prove connections between Saddam Hussein and Osama bin Laden in order to help justify the war in Iraq, the administration was ignoring the far more conclusive ties with Saudi Arabia. Those links are much stronger and far more troubling than has ever been previously disclosed, and until they are thoroughly investigated, the roots of al Qaeda's power, and the full story of 9/11, will never be known.

The connections between the Saudi government, particularly its intelligence service, and Osama bin Laden date back to the 1980s, when bin Laden, the seventeenth son of Saudi Arabia's richest and most successful construction magnate, first emerged as a young and enthusiastic sponsor of the Afghan resistance to the Soviet occupation, as well as of the Arab fighters pouring into Afghanistan to fight the So-

viets. At the time, bin Laden, Saudi intelligence, and even the CIA
had a common enemy in the Soviet Union, and Saudi intelligence
took special interest in the Arab foreign fighters joining in from
across the Middle East. Prince Turki al-Faisal, now the Saudi ambassador to the United States, is a member of the Saudi royal family who
served for roughly two decades as the chief of Saudi intelligence,
handling the Afghan account for Saudi Arabia. In the early and mid-
1980s, Prince Turki and his lieutenants had direct contact with bin
Laden. It is still unclear whether bin Laden was actually an agent of
Saudi intelligence during that period, but author Steve Coll, in *Ghost
Wars,* reported that bin Laden did have at the least a "substantial relationship" with Saudi intelligence during the Soviet war in Afghanistan.

What now seems clear is that Saudi intelligence found it difficult
to turn against bin Laden in the 1990s, as he evolved from an eccen-
tric supporter of anti-Communist freedom fighters into an anti-
American terrorist. Many Saudi intelligence officers sympathized
with his religious fundamentalism and his intense hatred for the
growing Western cultural influence over the Saudi kingdom. Even
after bin Laden was exiled, first to the Sudan and then to
Afghanistan, Saudi intelligence officials didn't see him as a major
threat to their interests until it was far too late. By the late 1990s, as al
Qaeda went on a terrorist rampage, the Saudis maintained an excru-
ciatingly complicated relationship with bin Laden, one that no
American official could ever fully understand.

There have been numerous signs, both large and small, that for
many years the sympathies of at least some officials in the Saudi security apparatus lay with Osama bin Laden and al Qaeda, and not with
the United States. When, for example, the CIA first created its
Osama bin Laden station in 1996 to begin to track and disrupt the
Saudi exile's activities, the agency asked the Saudis to provide copies
of Osama bin Laden's birth certificate, passport, bank records, and
other key records. Before the CIA could fully understand bin

Laden's intentions, agency officials believed they had to have better information about his background.

But the Saudis refused to turn over any of the documents, according to a CIA source. By the time of the 9/11 attacks, the CIA still had not received a copy of bin Laden's birth certificate from the government of Saudi Arabia, the source said.

In 1997, Saudi Arabia detained Sayed Tayib al-Madani, who had been a key financial aide to Osama bin Laden while bin Laden had been living in the Sudan. The CIA repeatedly asked the Saudis for access to al-Madani, because he knew virtually everything there was to know about al Qaeda's finances. It was said that, within al Qaeda, al-Madani had to approve every expenditure of more than $1,000. But the Saudis repeatedly refused, and the CIA didn't gain access to him until after the September 11 attacks, according to a CIA source.

"Before 9/11, the Saudis gave us almost nothing on al Qaeda," said one CIA source. In fact, in 1997, the CIA's bin Laden station issued a memorandum for CIA Director George Tenet, who was about to travel to Saudi Arabia, that identified the Saudi intelligence service as a "hostile service" on the issue of al Qaeda. Describing a foreign intelligence service as hostile means, at the very least, that they can not be trusted.

CIA sources also say that the agency has had strong evidence that some of the intelligence it has shared with Saudi security officials has ended up in the hands of al Qaeda operatives. For example, the CIA has in the past given the Saudis copies of NSA communications intercepts, which included conversations among suspected al Qaeda operatives in Saudi Arabia. But after the CIA gave the intercepts to the Saudis, the suspects quickly stopped using the communications that the Americans had been monitoring, making it far more difficult to track the terrorists.

Documents and computer files seized from al Qaeda operatives after 9/11 also revealed to the CIA that "al Qaeda had the run of

Saudi Arabia," as a CIA source familiar with the intelligence put it. That remained true, the source said, at least until May 2003, when the Saudis finally began to crack down.

Top Jordanian officials have also recounted a story to their American counterparts about Saudi sympathies to bin Laden that chilled the Americans who heard it. Because the Jordanian intelligence service, which is closely tied to the CIA, is renowned in the Middle East for its effectiveness, top Saudi officials asked it to review the Saudi intelligence apparatus and provide them with an assessment. When they began touring Saudi military and security facilities to conduct their review, however, the Jordanians saw something that helped explain why the Saudis had not done a better job in counterterrorism— a number of Saudi officials had Osama bin Laden screen savers on their office computers, according to an American source who heard the story from a top Jordanian official.

According to a former senior CIA official, the Saudi connection came into play in the spring of 1998, a time when America had perhaps its best chance to capture or kill Osama bin Laden before 9/11.

In early 1998, Osama bin Laden was still a relatively easy target; he did not yet seem to realize that he was under intense surveillance by the CIA, and so he stuck to a predictable schedule and lived a relatively stable existence. He spent most of his time in a rough compound called Tarnak Farms on the outskirts of Kandahar, Afghanistan, and regularly drove in a small convoy into Kandahar to meet with his Taliban hosts, including leader Mullah Omar. He talked on a satellite telephone and did not yet know that the NSA was eavesdropping on all of his conversations. True, he was living in one of the most remote regions of the world protected by armed bodyguards, and he enjoyed the full support of the Taliban government, but getting to bin Laden did not seem like an impossible task.

The CIA's bin Laden unit concluded that the Saudi exile could be taken, and came up with a plan under which local Pashtun tribesman working for the agency would capture him and hide him in a cave until the Americans came to claim him. A special CIA team would then fly into Afghanistan, retrieve bin Laden from the Afghans, and bring him back to face justice.

To be sure, the operation was high-risk, and there was a strong possibility that it would be so messy that bin Laden would be killed rather than captured. Tenet and the CIA's lawyers worried deeply about that issue; they believed that the covert action finding on al Qaeda that President Clinton had signed authorized only bin Laden's capture, not his death. (After 9/11, senior Clinton administration officials disputed Tenet's claim that he had never been given the authorization to kill bin Laden.)

Another problem was that the CIA was attempting a military-style operation, and, before 9/11, the CIA lacked much paramilitary capability. At the time, the U.S. military had no interest in getting drawn into Afghanistan in order to hunt for bin Laden, and so resisted White House efforts to get them to come up with plans of their own to target al Qaeda.

With the Pentagon out of the picture, the job was left to the agency. The CIA asked the U.S. Joint Special Operations Command to review its plan, conducted several field rehearsals, and had the plan vetted by the White House. While there was certainly no guarantee of success, the plan represented the U.S. government's best chance to grab Osama bin Laden before he might become a bigger threat.

Just as the final preparations for the operation were in the works, in May 1998, a delegation of top CIA officials, including Tenet, traveled to Saudi Arabia for meetings with Saudi Crown Prince Abdullah. According to a CIA source who was involved in the matter, Tenet asked the crown prince if the Saudis could help Washington deal with the problem of Osama bin Laden. The crown prince said yes, but only if the Americans kept this arrangement quiet. The CIA source said that the Saudi added that Washington should not ask that bin Laden be taken to the United States for trial. He could be dealt with by the Saudis. The Saudis proposed, in effect, to pay the Taliban for bin Laden.

Tenet sent a classified memorandum from Saudi Arabia back to Washington, addressed to National Security Advisor Sandy Berger, recommending that the CIA allow the Saudis to try to get bin Laden, according to a CIA source who later had access to the memo. Just as Tenet was maneuvering with the Saudis, he cancelled the CIA's own covert capture plan, convincing the White House that the agency should stand down. Within the CIA, one of the explanations given to senior officers involved in the operation was that the risk of killing bin Laden was too great, and the agency might then be accused of conducting an assassination.

The Saudis never seem to have made any serious attempt to get bin Laden. After Tenet's meeting with Crown Prince Abdullah, Prince Turki was sent to Afghanistan for a series of talks with the Taliban, but he wasn't able to reach an agreement with the Afghans about bin Laden. By then, the CIA's capture plan was dead, and the CIA had no other serious alternatives in the works. The agency's leaders had abandoned one of the only realistic opportunities the CIA ever had to capture bin Laden before 9/11. It is possible that the crown prince's offer of assistance simply provided Tenet and other top CIA officials an easy way out of a covert action plan that they had come to believe represented far too big of a gamble.

Of course, no one could have expected that the unintended consequences of the CIA's decision to trust the Saudis to go after bin Laden would become so apparent so quickly. In August 1998, less than three months after Tenet's visit to Saudi Arabia, suicide bombers blew up two U.S. embassies in East Africa, marking the start of a new and far more deadly phase in al Qaeda's war against the United States.

At about 4:30 in the morning on the frantic day after the East Africa bombings, George Tenet walked into the office of Michael Scheuer, then the chief of the bin Laden unit, and closed the door, according to Scheuer. Tenet seemed shaken; the decision to cancel the capture operation had quickly come back to haunt the agency. He looked at Scheuer and said, "I guess we made a mistake," Scheuer recalled later.

Scheuer, furious and blaming Tenet for the decision to kill the operation, responded: "No, sir, I think *you* made a mistake."

That December, Tenet wrote a memo declaring that the U.S. intelligence community was at war with al Qaeda. Almost no one saw the memo, and of those who did almost no one who really knew how the issue had been handled believed it.

The Saudis continued to drag their feet on investigating al Qaeda right up to the September 11 attacks, even as the CIA began to sense that a major attack was looming and was frantically asking the Saudis for assistance. Throughout the spring and summer of 2001, the CIA received a series of increasingly ominous reports that al Qaeda was planning a major terrorist attack. The problem was that the CIA did not know when or where the attacks were likely to take place. The best guess at the time was that al Qaeda was planning a strike somewhere overseas; all of its previous attacks against U.S. interests had been in the Middle East or Africa.

As part of its efforts that summer to uncover al Qaeda's plans, the CIA sought help from a number of foreign intelligence services, particularly in the Middle East, including that of Saudi Arabia. (Saudi Arabia has several security agencies, but the General Intelligence Directorate, or GID, is its main intelligence arm.)

Throughout that pre-9/11 period CIA headquarters sent the CIA station in Riyadh urgent NIACS—night action cables—seeking immediate, middle-of-the-night assistance from the Saudis on counterterrorism cases. No one at headquarters wanted to be the officer who allowed a case to wait until morning, only to find that an attack had taken place the night before.

Unfortunately, the CIA had little independent intelligence inside Saudi Arabia. It relied almost entirely on its liaison relationship with Saudi intelligence for information on Islamic extremists in the Saudi kingdom. But the Saudis were not being forthcoming despite the heightened alert conditions, and the CIA was not happy about it.

A small team of CIA officials went to Saudi Arabia that summer to complain about the lack of cooperation. The delegation traveled to Jedda, which Saudi officials preferred during the summer to the heat of the capital of Riyadh. The CIA officers pointedly reminded the Saudis that the CIA had begun to share much more intelligence with Saudi security—including highly classified communications intercepts of suspected terrorists, which the NSA had been reluctant to agree to hand over to the Saudis for fear that the information would be revealed to al Qaeda. And yet this new openness on the American side had not led to a similar increase in cooperation from the Saudi side.

A number of current and former CIA officials say they believe that the Saudis simply couldn't bring themselves to go after al Qaeda before 9/11. The Saudi government seemed convinced that it was better to appease Islamic extremists than provoke them. In addition, there were strong suspicions among some CIA officials that at least some of the intelligence they shared with Saudi security officials was passed on to al Qaeda operatives.

The story of Abu Zubaydah's capture, and his links to Saudi Arabia, did not end with his pocket litter. After he was seized in Pakistan, Abu Zubaydah was flown to Thailand and was placed in a secret

CIA detention facility. At some point after his capture, U.S. sources say that the CIA created an atmosphere that allowed them to convince Abu Zubaydah that he was in Saudi Arabia, in the custody off Saudi intelligence. The CIA believed that he would be so frightened by the prospect of being tortured at the hands of the Saudis that he would begin to talk.

Instead, the American officers were surprised that Abu Zubaydah was actually pleased and relieved to be in Saudi custody. As Gerald Posner has written, Abu Zubaydah then gave his captors several phone numbers of Saudi contacts who could vouch for him and who could help him out of his predicament.

(In addition to the incidents described by Posner, a senior former American government official said that the United States has obtained other evidence that suggests connections between al Qaeda operatives and telephone numbers associated with Saudi officials.)

There is no conclusive evidence that members of the Saudi royal family or other senior Saudi officials had direct connections to Abu Zubaydah, but the fact that the terrorist leader gave his interrogators those numbers raises intriguing questions.

Some officials believed that Abu Zubaydah's recitation of the Saudi telephone numbers may have been part of a well-rehearsed disinformation campaign, to be employed in the event of capture and designed to sow discord between America and its allies. After all, Osama bin Laden hated the Saudi royal family and believed that they were corrupt autocrats who had defiled Islam's holy places by inviting American troops onto Saudi soil following the first Gulf War.

There is no evidence that a thorough examination of his claims of ties to powerful Saudis was ever conducted.

Both before and after 9/11, the CIA continued to rely almost entirely on the Saudi security services for information about Islamic extremists operating inside Saudi Arabia, and had almost no spies of its own inside Saudi Arabia who could report on the Saudi relationship with al Qaeda.

Some CIA sources say that George Tenet set the tone for the CIA's Saudi relationship by relying heavily on developing close relationships with top Saudi officials, including Prince Bandar bin Sultan bin Abdulaziz, then the Saudi ambassador to the United States. Tenet met regularly with the Saudi ambassador. CIA officers familiar with the agency's relationship with Saudi Arabia say that about once a month, Tenet would slip away from CIA headquarters and travel to Bandar's nearby estate in McLean, Virginia, for quiet talks. (In a 2003 profile of Bandar in *The New Yorker*, Elsa Walsh wrote that Tenet showed up at Bandar's home while she was interviewing the Saudi.)

"Bandar and Tenet had a very close relationship," said one CIA officer. "Bandar had a unique role, he was in charge of the American relationship for Saudi Arabia."

But some CIA officers handling Saudi issues complain that Tenet would not tell them what he had discussed with Bandar, making it difficult for agency officials to know the nature of any deals their boss was arranging with the Saudis. They would usually find out what Tenet had said to Bandar only much later, and then only from the Saudis.

Tenet considered the Saudi relationship so sensitive that in the late 1990s, he named one of his closest aides to be Riyadh station chief. While the former aide was station chief in Saudi Arabia, he would sometimes communicate directly with Tenet, skirting others in the chain of command within the Near East Division, according to CIA sources. "That drove the barons of the NE and CTC [Counterterrorism Center] crazy because they were not in the loop," recalled one CIA source.

Separately, a veteran CIA analyst said that top agency officials sought to prevent analysts from writing intelligence reports that raised questions about the vulnerabilities faced by the Saudi regime from Islamic extremism, and that as a result, the CIA never adequately addressed the most pressing issues concerning the future of the Saudi kingdom. Top CIA managers were intent on making sure that the CIA did not produce politically inconvenient intelligence that could cause headaches at the White House, the longtime Middle East analyst believed.

Of course, the Saudis had much more powerful allies in official Washington than George Tenet and the CIA. Prince Bandar, for example, was extremely close to the first President Bush and the entire Bush family; in his book about the war in Iraq, *Plan of Attack,* Bob Woodward reported that President Bush alerted Bandar to the timing of the 2003 invasion before he notified Secretary of State Colin Powell.

Bandar's close ties to the White House, the State Department, and the CIA helped the Saudi elite avoid serious scrutiny of potential links to Islamic extremists. When a joint House-Senate inquiry into the September 11 attacks uncovered evidence that Bandar's wife had provided tens of thousands of dollars that ended up in the hands of the family of a Saudi man in San Diego who had aided two of the September 11 hijackers, most of official Washington rallied around Bandar and his wife and accepted without further inquiry the official Saudi explanation that it was simply charity.

Washington's failure to confront questions about Saudi Arabia before and after 9/11 raises much broader questions, including whether the Bush administration really understands or knows how to deal with the rapid political change now under way throughout the Middle East.

There is no doubt that something new and bracing is under way in the region; unprecedented elections in 2005 in Iraq and in the Palestinian territories were followed by mass demonstrations in Beirut against Syrian control over Lebanon's government, which ultimately forced the withdrawal of the Syrian military from the country. Saudi Arabia even held municipal elections, a small step toward political reform in the monarchy.

The sudden burst of democracy throughout the Middle East, where corrupt dictatorships and monarchies have dominated the political landscape for generations, arrived like a badly needed breath of fresh air. For the Bush administration—in search of a new justification for the war in Iraq after the failure to find Iraq's weapons of mass destruction or any evidence of a terrorist alliance between Iraq and al Qaeda—the climate of political reform early in 2005 brought a new sense of vindication for the decision to topple Saddam Hussein.

President Bush does deserve credit for making the spread of democracy in the Middle East a centerpiece of his agenda for his second term. His second inaugural speech in January 2005, in which he laid out a sweeping vision of a global democratic future, resonated with Arab professionals and the growing middle class, particularly among the generation of young Arabs who have been deeply frustrated by the political and economic limits they confront. The young dissidents have been aided by new information technologies, from cell phones to text messaging to the Internet to satellite television news, which has made it virtually impossible for autocratic regimes to staunch political debate and dissent. The same Internet cafes in Arab cities that allow Islamic terrorists to communicate undetected also give new freedom to dissidents.

But the Bush administration's biggest problems have come when it has ignored the realities of the Middle East, has accepted tainted and overly optimistic intelligence, and has suppressed contrary views within its own government. These problems have compounded the CIA's own failures. In the case of one operation in particular—an operation run during the last year of the Clinton administration and later endorsed by the Bush administration—the consequences are frightening. Against Iran, CIA decision makers overrode objections and played an extraordinarily dangerous game. It is a game that Bush administration officials say they may want to play again, despite the risks.

9

A ROGUE OPERATION

S HE HAD PROBABLY done this a dozen times before. Modern digital technology had made clandestine communications with overseas agents seem routine. Back in the Cold War, contacting a secret
agent in Moscow or Beijing was a dangerous, labor-intensive process
that could take days or even weeks to arrange. But by 2004, it was
possible to send high-speed, encrypted messages directly and instan-
taneously from CIA headquarters to agents in the field who were
equipped with small, covert personal communications devices. So
the officer at CIA headquarters assigned to handle communications
with the agency's spies in Iran probably didn't think twice when she
began her latest download. With a few simple commands, she sent a
secret data flow to one of the Iranian agents in the CIA's spy network.
Just like she had done so many times before.

But this time, the ease and speed of the technology betrayed her.
The CIA officer had made a disastrous mistake. She had sent information to one Iranian agent meant for an entire spy network; the
data could be used to identify virtually every spy the CIA had inside
Iran.

Mistake piled on mistake. As the CIA later learned, the Iranian
who received the download was actually a double agent. The agent
quickly turned the data over to Iranian security officials, and it enabled them to "roll up" the CIA's agent network throughout Iran.

CIA sources say that several of the Iranian agents were arrested and jailed, while the fates of some of the others is still unknown.

This espionage disaster, of course, was not reported in the press. It left the CIA virtually blind in Iran, unable to provide any significant intelligence on one of the most critical issues facing the United States—whether Tehran was about to go nuclear.

In fact, just as President Bush and his aides were making the case in 2004 and 2005 that Iran was moving rapidly to develop nuclear weapons, the American intelligence community found itself unable to provide the evidence to back up the administration's public arguments. On the heels of the CIA's failure to provide accurate prewar intelligence on Iraq's weapons of mass destruction, the agency was once again clueless in the Middle East. In the spring of 2005, in the wake of the CIA's Iranian disaster, Porter Goss, the CIA's new director, told President Bush in a White House briefing that the CIA really didn't know how close Iran was to becoming a nuclear power.

The Bush administration has never publicly disclosed the extent to which it is now operating in the blind on Iran. But deep in the bowels of the CIA, someone must be nervously, but very privately, wondering: *Whatever happened to those nuclear blueprints we gave to the Iranians?*

The story dates back to the Clinton administration and February 2000, when one frightened Russian scientist walked Vienna's winter streets. Enveloped by the February cold, he dodged the bright red and white Strassenbahn, the quaint electric tramcars that roll in slow circuits around the city, while he debated whether to go through with his secret mission.

I'm not a spy, he thought to himself. *I'm a scientist. What am I doing here?*

He fingered the package stuffed in his overcoat, making certain the priceless documents were still there and that this crazy job wasn't just a bad dream.

The Russian pulled the note out of his pocket, looked at the address one more time, and then plowed ahead, confused. He knew nothing about Vienna and quickly found himself lost along the operatic city's broad avenues. Was he looking for something called Rueppgasse, or was it called Heinestrasse? Was he supposed to take Strassenbahn 21? He rode two full circuits on the S-Bahn 21 train, searching in vain for the right stop. Should he switch to the U-Bahn, Vienna's subway? The Permanent Mission of the Islamic Republic of Iran to the International Atomic Energy Agency (IAEA) wasn't the easiest office in Vienna to find.

They could have at least given me good directions.

As he stumbled along into Vienna's north end, in the unglamorous neighborhood surrounding the Praterstern U-Bahn station, the same question pounded in his brain again and again, but he couldn't find an answer.

What was the CIA thinking?

The Russian had good reason to be afraid. He was walking around Vienna with blueprints for a nuclear bomb.

To be precise, he was carrying technical designs for a TBA 480 high-voltage block, otherwise known as a "firing set," for a Russian-designed nuclear weapon. He held in his hands knowledge needed to create a perfect implosion that could trigger a nuclear chain reaction inside a small spherical core. It was one of the greatest engineering secrets in the world, providing the solution to one of a handful of problems that separated nuclear powers such as the United States and Russia from the rogue countries like Iran that were desperate to join the nuclear club but had so far fallen short.

He still couldn't believe the orders he had received from CIA headquarters. The CIA had given him the nuclear blueprints and then sent him to Vienna to sell them—or simply give them—to the Iranian representatives to the IAEA. With the Russian doing

Langley's bidding, the CIA appeared to be about to help Iran leapfrog one of the last remaining engineering hurdles blocking its path to a nuclear weapon. The dangerous irony was not lost on the Russian—the IAEA was an international organization created to restrict the spread of nuclear technology. The IAEA's Vienna headquarters, inside the United Nation's sprawling concrete compound, a jumble of geometric-shaped buildings assembled like a Christmas pile of children's toys along the Danube River just outside the city center, was the leading forum for international debate over the proliferation of nuclear weapons technology. It was the place where the United States came to level charges against rogue nations such as Iran and North Korea over their clandestine nuclear programs. IAEA experts traveled the world to try to police the use of nuclear power, to make certain that peaceful energy-generation programs weren't providing cover for the clandestine development of nuclear weapons. In 2005, the IAEA and its chief, Mohamed ElBaradei, would win the Nobel Peace Prize for their counter proliferation efforts.

But in 2000, the CIA was coming to Vienna to stage an operation that could help one of the most dangerous regimes in the world obtain a nuclear weapon.

The Russian stood out like a poor eastern cousin on Vienna's jeweled cityscape.

He was a nuclear engineer who had defected to the United States years earlier and quietly settled in America. He went through the CIA's defector resettlement program and endured long debriefings in which CIA experts and scientists from the national laboratories tried to drain him of everything he knew about the status of Russia's nuclear weapons program. Like many other Russian defectors before him, his tiresome complaints about money and status had gained him a reputation within the CIA of being difficult to manage. But he was too valuable for the CIA to toss away.

One secret CIA report said that the Russian "was a known handling problem due to his demanding and overbearing nature." Yet the same report stated that he was also a "sensitive asset" who could be used in a "high-priority covert-action operation."

So despite their disputes, the CIA had arranged for the Russian to become an American citizen and had kept him on the payroll, to the tune of $5,000 a month. It really did seem like easy money, with few strings attached. Life was good. He was happy to be on the CIA gravy train.

Until now. The CIA was placing him on the front lines of a plan that seemed to be completely at odds with the interests of the United States, and it had taken a lot of persuading by his CIA case officer to convince him to go through with what appeared to be a rogue operation.

The case officer worked hard to convince him—even though the officer had doubts about the plan as well. As he was sweet-talking the Russian into flying to Vienna, the case officer wondered whether he was being set up by CIA management, in some dark political or bureaucratic game that he didn't understand. Was he involved in an illegal covert action? Should he expect to be hauled before a congressional committee and grilled because he was the officer who helped give nuclear blueprints to Iran? The code name for this operation was MERLIN; to the officer, that seemed like a wry tip-off that nothing about this program was what it appeared to be. He did his best to hide his concerns from his Russian agent.

The Russian's assignment from the CIA was to pose as an unemployed and greedy scientist who was willing to sell his soul—and the secrets of the atomic bomb—to the highest bidder. By hook or by crook, the CIA told him, he was to get the nuclear blueprints to the Iranians. They would quickly recognize their value and rush them back to their superiors in Tehran.

The plan had been laid out for the defector during a CIA-financed trip to San Francisco, where he had meetings with CIA officers and nuclear experts mixed in with leisurely wine-tasting trips to Sonoma Country. In a luxurious San Francisco hotel room, a senior CIA official involved in the operation walked the Russian through the details of the plan. He brought in experts from one of the national laboratories to go over the blueprints that he was supposed to give the Iranians.

The senior CIA officer could see that the Russian was nervous, and so he tried to downplay the significance of what they were asking him to do. He told the Russian that the CIA was mounting the operation simply to find out where the Iranians are with their nuclear program. This was just an intelligence-gathering effort, the CIA officer said, not an illegal attempt to give Iran the bomb. He suggested that the Iranians already had the technology he was going to hand over to them. It was all a game. Nothing too serious.

The Russian reluctantly agreed, but he was still clearly suspicious of the CIA's motives.

He was afraid because he fully understood the value of the information he was supposed to pass to the Iranians. He certainly understood it better than did his CIA handlers. Before he defected, he had worked as an engineer at Arzamas-16, the original center of the Soviet nuclear weapons program and the Russian equivalent of Los Alamos, the home of the Manhattan Project. Founded in 1946, when Soviet dictator Joseph Stalin was rushing to catch up with the Americans and trying to turn the Soviet Union into a nuclear power, Arzamas-16 had once been so secret that it was known only as the "installation" or the "site." Built on the grounds of a czarist-era monastery, about 400 kilometers from Moscow at the old town of Sarova, the complex's first name was Arzamas-60, since it was 60 kilometers from the town of Arzamas; but the Soviets realized that name was too revealing about its location, so they changed it to Arzamas-16. In 1947, the entire city of Sarov officially disappeared from Russian maps.

Arzamas-16 was where the Soviets built their first atomic and hydrogen bombs, and today, 30,000 people still work at nuclear weapons–related facilities located within a restricted area in the heavily guarded Arzamas-16 district. It wasn't until 1995 that Russian President Boris Yeltsin changed its name back to Sarov.

After the collapse of the Soviet Union, the United States feared that poverty-stricken scientists from Arzamas-16 and other facilities like it would be tempted to work for Iraq, North Korea—or Iran. Weapons proliferation really meant the spread of scientific knowledge and the spread of scientists.

The end of the Cold War meant the end of regular paychecks for Russian nuclear scientists, and there was a real danger that Russian technical expertise would spread like a virus to the totalitarian states of the third world. In the 1990s, in fact, the director of one Russian nuclear institute killed himself, reportedly over the government's failure to meet his payroll. There were Russian press accounts of uranium being stolen from Arzamas-16. What was to stop underpaid Russian scientists from walking off with technical expertise, and perhaps the blueprints and even the fissile material needed to help rogue states build a bomb?

Fortunately, at just the right moment, two centrist American senators, one Democrat and one Republican, saw the danger and came up with one of the most farsighted U.S. foreign relations programs since the Marshall Plan. In 1991, Sam Nunn, a Georgia Democrat and the party's leading voice on national security, and Richard Lugar, a cautious Republican and former mayor of Indianapolis who had turned himself into a foreign affairs specialist in the Senate, crafted legislation that helped prevent a massive drain of nuclear technology out of the former Soviet Union. Known as the Nunn-Lugar Cooperative Threat Reduction Program, the legislation created joint U.S.-Russian programs to deactivate thousands of nuclear warheads in the former Soviet Union, and helped rid the Ukraine, Kazakhstan, and Belarus of the nuclear weapons they had inherited at the time of the breakup of the Soviet Union.

Equally important was Nunn-Lugar's impact on the lives of

Russian scientists. Nunn-Lugar helped more than twenty thousand Russian experts involved in Soviet weapons programs find alternative, and more peaceful, forms of research. Arzamas-16 even forged new, cooperative ties with Los Alamos. By 1993, Los Alamos and Sarov were officially sister cities.

Behind the public face of Nunn-Lugar, the CIA was also doing its part, quietly helping Russian nuclear scientists to defect and resettle in the United States, rather than go to Iran or Iraq, providing them new lives and enough money to keep their talents off the open market. It was this CIA defector program that brought the Russian to the United States.

But now, the CIA was no longer keeping the Russian engineer off the nuclear market, nor was it keeping Russian know-how under wraps. The blueprints the Russian was to hand over to the Iranians were originally from the Arzamas complex, brought to the CIA by another defector.

What better way for the CIA to hide its involvement in this operation than to have a veteran of Arzamas personally hand over the Russian nuclear designs?

His CIA case officer had coached the Russian as best he could on how to make contact with the Iranians. It wasn't easy; you don't just look up the address for the covert Iranian nuclear weapons program in the Yellow Pages. Still, maybe there was a way you could make contact on the Internet. Maybe it really was as simple as sending out e-mail.

At the case officer's urging, the Russian started sending messages to Iranian scientists, scholars, and even Iranian diplomats stationed at the IAEA in Vienna. In his e-mails, he would explain that he had information of great interest to Iran and that he was seeking a meeting with someone who could hear him out. The messages were designed to be playfully intriguing, but not quite revealing. Just enough to prompt a response.

He also started attending academic conferences in the United

States attended by Iranian-American scientists. These conferences sometimes attracted scientists visiting from Iran, and they might be good contacts. The Russian stood out like a sore thumb among the Iranian academics, but that was the point. He wanted people to notice him. He was a nuclear salesman, ready for business.

Of course, it wasn't unusual for Russian and Iranian scientists to mix, and that was another point the CIA was counting on. There was a well-established channel of Russian technical support for Iran's nuclear power generation program. Moscow had an $800 million contract to help Iran build a light water reactor at Bushehr. The United States had publicly complained that Iran was using Bushehr and the country's commercial nuclear program to advance its nuclear weapons development efforts. American officials, in both the Clinton and Bush administrations, consistently asked why Iran needed a nuclear power program when it had so much oil and natural gas; in one State Department statement, Washington noted that Iran annually flares off more natural gas than Bushehr could produce. For at least a decade, a key sticking point in U.S.-Russian diplomatic relations has been Russia's ties to Iran and Moscow's willingness to view Iran as an eager customer for Russian arms, rather than as a growing strategic threat in the Middle East.

With Tehran serving as a major shopping bazaar for Russia's post–Cold War arms sales, it certainly wasn't unusual to find Russian and Iranian technicians and bureaucrats mingling. The Russian defector could exploit that tendency to make inroads with the Iranians.

As he mingled with the scientists and other academics, the Russian picked up business cards and e-mail addresses. The Russian began to e-mail his new contacts, sending intriguing messages explaining that he wanted to talk with them about his ability to provide materials of interest to Iran. Finally, at one conference, he hit pay dirt when he met a physics professor visiting from Tehran.

After the CIA checked out his background, the agency decided that the contact with the Iranian professor was promising. The CIA hoped the Iranian academic might serve as the Russian's entrée into the secret world of Tehran's nuclear program. At the least, he might be able to put the Russian in contact with the right people in Iran.

The Russian followed up his chance encounter with e-mails to the scientist back at his university in Iran. The Russian explained that he had information that was extremely important, and he wanted to make an offer. After some delays, the Iranian finally responded, with a wary message, asking what he had in mind.

That was enough for the CIA. Now the Russian could tell Iranian officials in Vienna that he had been in touch with a respected scientist in Tehran before he showed up on their doorstep.

The CIA had discovered that a high-ranking Iranian official would be traveling to Vienna and visiting the Iranian mission to the IAEA, and so the agency decided to take the next step and send the Russian to Vienna at the same time. It was hoped that he could make contact with either the Iranian ambassador to the IAEA or the visitor from Tehran.

The CIA sent him to Vienna without any backup. Langley didn't want to risk exposure. The CIA station in Vienna wasn't asked to play any role to support the Russian; this operation was dubbed a "special access program," and its existence was a tightly held secret. Only a handful of CIA officers knew of the existence of MERLIN. Better to let the Russian get lost and fumble his way around town than tell more officers about the operation. Sending him to Vienna without any minders would also convince anyone watching that he was just what he appeared to be—an amateur at this game, freelancing.

The Russian's cover story was that he was the go-between for the other Russian scientist who had brought the nuclear blueprints out of Arzamas. In truth, he had never met the other defector, but that didn't matter. The story would help answer any questions the Iranians might have about how he came to acquire the blueprints, which were not easy to access or remove from Arzamas.

The Russian was also told not to try to hide the fact that he now lived in the United States. His story should be as close to the truth as possible. Just because he was living in America didn't mean he was working for the CIA.

But now that he was in Vienna, he was playing the role of bumbling scientist too well, unable to find the Iranian mission, uncertain even where to get off the train. "I spent a lot of time to ask people as I could [language problem] and they told me that no streets with this name are around," the Russian later explained to the CIA, in his imperfect English.

Maybe deep down, he didn't want to get off the tram, and didn't want to find the right office. He had to find time to think.

He could not stop thinking about his trip to San Francisco, when he had studied the blueprints the CIA had given him. Within minutes of being handed the designs, he had identified a flaw. "This isn't right," he told the CIA officers gathered around the hotel room. "There is something wrong." His comments prompted stony looks, but no straight answers from the CIA men in the room. No one in the San Francisco meeting seemed surprised by the Russian's assertion that the blueprints didn't look quite right, but no one wanted to enlighten him further on the matter, either.

In fact, the CIA case officer who was the Russian's personal handler had been stunned by the Russian's statement. During a break, he took the senior CIA officer aside. "He wasn't supposed to know that," the CIA case officer told his superior. "He wasn't supposed to find a flaw."

"Don't worry," the senior CIA officer calmly replied. "It doesn't matter."

The CIA case officer couldn't believe the senior CIA officer's answer, but he still managed to keep his fears from the Russian, and he continued to train him for his mission.

After their trip to San Francisco, the case officer handed the Russian a sealed envelope with the nuclear blueprints inside. The Russian was told not to open the envelope under any circumstances. He was to follow the CIA's instructions to find the Iranians and give them the envelope with the documents inside. Keep it simple, and get out of Vienna safe and alive, the Russian was told. But the defector was more worried than ever about what kind of game the CIA was getting him into. And he had his own ideas about how he might play that game.

In Vienna, the Russian went over his options one more time and made a decision. He unsealed the envelope with the nuclear blueprints and included a personal letter of his own to the Iranians. No matter what the CIA told him, he was going to hedge his bets. There was obviously something wrong with these blueprints—so he decided to mention that fact to the Iranians in his letter. They would certainly find flaws for themselves, and if he didn't tell them first, they would never want to deal with him again. In his badly broken English, the Russian addressed the Iranians as if they were academic colleagues. He later gave a copy of his letter to the CIA.

> *To University:*
> *First, let me introduce myself. I am a person, who worked for many years in atomic industry. Please check out next page for my personal info please.*
>
> *I would like to inform you I have very valuable information about design and production of atomic weapon. At this time I possess a description of one of key elements of modern system, TBA 480 high-voltage automatic block. Described device is known as a fire switch which lets to initiate simultaneously all detonators at a weapon core (spherical charge). I am sure other devices can be available for your review in the future. I did not contact right people in your country di-*

rectly because unfortunately I could not find them. Of course, I tried many other ways to attract attention to this info by telling little bit about what I have but it does not work. Whole misunderstanding, and accordingly wasting time and disappointing. So I decided to offer this absolutely real and valuable basic information for free now and you can evaluate that. Also I sent e-mail to inform [the Iranian professor] about this possible event. Please let him know you have this package.

What is purpose of my offer?

If you try to create a similar device you will need to ask some practical questions. No problem. You will get answers but I expect to be paid for that. Let's talk about details later when I see a real interest in it.

Now just take your time for professional study of enclosed documentation. My contact info on next page.

The Russian was thus warning the Iranians as carefully as he could that there was a flaw somewhere in the nuclear blueprints, and he could help them find it. At the same time, he was still going through with the CIA's operation in the only way he thought would work.

The Russian slid his letter in with the blueprints and resealed the envelope.

After his day of floundering around Vienna, the Russian returned to his hotel, near the city's large Stadtpark. He did a computer search and found the right street address for the Iranian mission. His courage bolstered, he decided he would go back and finish the job in the morning.

By 8:00 A.M., he found 19 Heinstrasse, a five-story office and apartment building with a flat, pale green and beige façade in a quiet, slightly down-at-the-heels neighborhood in Vienna's north end. The street was crowded with tobacco shops, bars, and cafes, a tanning salon, even a strip club. Now the Russian realized why he had missed it; there was no sign announcing the Iranian mission. The only proof that this was the right place was a mail directory, with three rows of tenants' names on the wall beside the building's front door. Amid the list of Austrian tenants, there was one simple line: "PM/Iran." The Iranians clearly didn't want publicity.

The Russian's fevered rush of adrenaline as he approached the building suddenly cooled when he realized the Iranian office was closed for the day for some unexplained reason. Once again, he spent the day walking Vienna, and once again mulling over the CIA's orders. He returned to his hotel again that night, still clutching the undelivered documents.

He returned one last time to the Iranian mission early the next morning and stood for a few agonizing minutes on the empty sidewalk outside.

He came back that afternoon, and an Austrian postman finally helped him make up his mind. As the Russian stood silently by, the postman opened the building door, dropped off the mail, and walked quietly away to complete his neighborhood rounds. His courage finally reinforced, the Russian decided to follow suit; he now realized that he could leave his package without actually having to talk to anyone. He slipped through the front door, and hurriedly shoved his envelope through the inner door slot at the Iranian office.

"At 1:30 P.M. I got a chance to be inside of the gate," at the entrance to the Iranian mission, the Russian later explained in writing to the CIA. "They have two mailboxes: one after gate on left side for post mail (I could not open it without key) and other one nearby an internal door to the mission. Last one has easy access to insert mail and also it was locked. I passed internal door and reached the mission entry door and put a package inside their mailbox on left side of their door. I cover it old newspaper but if somebody wants that is possible to remove this package from mailbox, in my opinion. I had no choice."

The Russian fled the mission without being seen. He was deeply relieved that he had finally made the handoff without ever having to come face to face with a real live Iranian. He flew back to the United

States without being detected by either Austrian security or, more important, by Iranian intelligence.

From its headquarters at Fort Meade, Maryland, the National Security Agency monitors global airline reservation databases, constantly checking on the travel arrangements of foreign officials and others targeted by American intelligence around the world. In February 2000, the NSA was also eavesdropping on the telephone lines of the Iranian mission in Vienna. It could intercept communications between the mission and Tehran. In addition, the NSA had broken the codes of the Ministry of Intelligence and Security, Iran's foreign intelligence service. The Americans had several different ways to track the movements of Iranian officials in and out of Vienna.

Just days after the Russian dropped off his package at the Iranian mission, the NSA reported that an Iranian official in Vienna abruptly changed his schedule and suddenly made airline reservations and flew home to Iran. The odds were that the nuclear blueprints were now in Tehran.

The Russian scientist's fears about the operation were well founded. He was the front man for what may have been one of the most reckless operations in the modern history of the CIA, one that may have helped put nuclear weapons in the hands of a charter member of what President George W. Bush has called the "axis of evil."

Operation MERLIN has been one of the most closely guarded secrets in the Clinton and Bush administrations. And it may not be over. Some officials have suggested that it might be repeated against other countries.

* * *

MERLIN was born out of frustration. For more than a decade, one post–Cold War CIA director after another went before Congress and the nation to vow that America's spies were now focused on new, gathering threats posed by a set of "hard targets." Terrorists. Rogue nations. Weapons of mass destruction. Each new director promised that the CIA was changing rapidly to adapt to this complex new world in which the Soviet Union was no longer the main enemy. But the CIA has failed in its new mission and has never found out enough about any of these new targets. Iran's nuclear program remains one of the most impenetrable of them all.

Even before the disastrous collapse of its Iranian spy network in 2004, the CIA was able to pick up only fragmentary information about Iran's nuclear program. Officials who are critical of the CIA's efforts say that the agency's counterproliferation programs have relied far too heavily on intelligence collected from technical methods—spy satellites, eavesdropping, and code breaking, as well as "measurement and signature" intelligence, which includes the collection and analysis of data from hidden equipment like remote ground sensors. Lacking definitive answers about Iran's atomic program, the CIA has instead offered a series of safe and cautious estimates. Over the years, the agency has repeatedly stated that Iran was within five to ten years of becoming a nuclear power. Those five to ten years keep stretching and expanding.

The Counterproliferation Division within the CIA's Directorate of Operations, the agency's clandestine espionage arm, came up with MERLIN and other clandestine operations as creative, if unorthodox, ways to try to penetrate Tehran's nuclear development program. In some cases, the CIA has worked jointly with Israeli intelligence on such operations, according to people familiar with the convert program. None are known to have worked.

One bizarre plan called for the sabotage of Iran's electrical grid in areas of the country near its secret nuclear installations. The CIA conducted tests of the electrical sabotage equipment at the U.S. government's Nevada nuclear test range. The plan called for an electromagnetic pulse device that could be smuggled into Iran and then hidden next to large power transmission lines carrying electricity into the country's nuclear facilities. The CIA would later remotely detonate the device, which would send a massive electrical pulse down the power lines, shorting out the computer systems inside the Iranian nuclear complex.

The CIA worked with Mossad, Israel's spy service, on the plan, and Mossad agents volunteered to smuggle the devices into Iran. The Israelis told the CIA that they had Iranian agents who would carry out the plan on their behalf.

But there were major technical problems that made the plan unworkable. The electromagnetic devices were so large that they had to be carried in a large truck, and then parked next to the power lines; the CIA realized that was impossible.

Then there was MERLIN. On paper, MERLIN was supposed to stunt the development of Tehran's nuclear program by sending Iran's weapons experts down the wrong technical path. The CIA believed that once the Iranians had the blueprints and studied them, they would believe the designs were usable and so would start to build an atom bomb based on the flawed designs. But Tehran would get a big surprise when its scientists tried to explode their new bomb. Instead of a mushroom cloud, the Iranian scientists would witness a disappointing fizzle. The Iranian nuclear program would suffer a humiliating setback, and Tehran's goal of becoming a nuclear power would have been delayed by several years. In the meantime, the CIA, by watching Iran's reaction to the blueprints, would have gained a wealth of information about the status of Iran's weapons program, which has been shrouded in secrecy.

It's not clear who originally came up with the idea, but the plan was first approved by President Bill Clinton. After the Russian scientist's fateful trip to Vienna, however, the MERLIN operation was endorsed by the Bush administration, possibly with an eye toward repeating it against North Korea or other dangerous states.

The CIA had obtained genuine Russian nuclear weapons blueprints from a Russian scientist and had forwarded them to one of the national laboratories—almost certainly Sandia National Laboratories in New Mexico—to be scrutinized by American nuclear experts. Sandia, in Albuquerque, is one of the jewels in the crown of the American nuclear establishment. Its origins were in the so-called Z Division of the Los Alamos National Laboratory during the Manhattan Project. Z Division conducted the engineering and design work for the nonnuclear portions of the first atomic bomb, including the weapons assembly. Sandia thus houses the U.S. government's institutional memory for how a nuclear bomb is put together.

Scientists at the national laboratory were asked to implant flaws into the Russian blueprints. The flaws were supposed to be so clever and well hidden that no one could detect their presence.

Next, the agency needed to figure out how to get the designs to the Iranians without Tehran realizing that the blueprints were coming from the CIA.

That job was assigned to the CIA's Counterproliferation Division. The CPD chose the Russian defector.

That was the idea behind MERLIN, anyway. But like so many of the CIA's other recent operations, this one didn't go according to plan. First, of course, the Russian spotted flaws in the blueprints. Second, the CIA never maintained adequate controls over the nuclear blueprints—or over the Russian. The Russian was supposed to believe that he was handing over genuine nuclear designs. Instead, his cover letter may have convinced the Iranians to be wary of the blueprints. Furthermore, the CIA also gave the blueprints to the Iranians without any certain way of monitoring their use by Iranian scientists. The CIA was flying blind—dangerously so. In effect, the CIA asked the Russian to throw the blueprints over the transom, and then the agency just hoped for the best.

Several former CIA officials say that the theory behind MERLIN—handing over tainted weapons designs to confound one of America's adversaries—is a trick that has been used many times in past operations, stretching back to the Cold War. But in previous cases, such Trojan horse operations involved conventional weapons; none of the former officials had ever heard of the CIA attempting to conduct this kind of high-risk operation with designs for a nuclear bomb. The former officials also said these kind of programs must be closely monitored by senior CIA managers in order to control the flow of information to the adversary. If mishandled, they could easily help an enemy accelerate its weapons development.

That may be what happened with MERLIN.

The CIA case officer was deeply concerned by the ease with which the Russian had discovered flaws in the designs. He knew that that meant the Iranians could, too, and that they could then fix and make use of the repaired blueprints to help them build a bomb. If so, the CIA would have assisted the Iranians in joining the nuclear club. He grew so concerned about whether he had aided the Iranian nuclear program that he went to the Senate Select Committee on Intelligence to tell congressional investigators about the problems with the program. But no action was ever taken.

For his part, the Russian never understood why the CIA wanted him to give the Iranians blueprints that contained such obvious mistakes. It made no sense. And so he wrote the Iranians his personal letter.

It is not known whether the Russian ever communicated again with the Iranians, or whether they tried to contact him. But after receiving his letter warning them that they would need further help to make the blueprints useful, it is entirely possible that the Iranians showed the plans to other experts familiar with Russian nuclear designs and thereby identified the defects.

Iran has spent nearly twenty years trying to develop nuclear weapons, and in the process has created a strong base of sophisticated scientists knowledgeable enough to spot flaws in nuclear blueprints. What's more, the Iranians have received extensive support for years from Russian and Chinese nuclear experts who could help the Iranians review the material. In addition, Tehran also obtained nuclear blueprints from the black-market network of Pakistani scientist A. Q. Khan, and so already had workable blueprints against which to compare the designs obtained from the CIA.

Even if the Iranians were interested in using the blueprints provided by the mysterious Russian, they would certainly examine and test the data in the documents before ever actually trying to build a bomb. Nuclear experts say that they would thus be able to extract valuable information from the blueprints while ignoring the flaws.

"If a country of seventy million inhabitants [Iran], with quite a good scientific and technical community, got [nuclear documents with supposedly hidden flaws], they might learn something," warned a nuclear weapons expert with the IAEA. "If [the flaw] is bad enough, they will find it quite quickly. That would be my fear."

MERLIN has been conducted in the darkest corner of the American national security establishment at one of the most significant moments in the long and bitter history of U.S.-Iran relations. Iran has bedeviled American presidents since Jimmy Carter and the embassy hostage crisis, and neither Bill Clinton nor George W. Bush have based their policies on an adequate understanding of the volatile political dynamics under way in Iran.

Throughout the late 1990s, the Clinton administration was convinced that political reformers and youthful moderates were ascendant in Iran, and so the White House twisted itself in knots trying to open back-channel talks with Tehran. But in order to reach out to the Iranians, Clinton had to downplay evidence that Tehran was still the world's leading state sponsor of terrorism, that Iran was still an Islamic republic whose security apparatus was controlled by powerful, conservative mullahs who wanted nothing to do with the United States, and that the Iranian regime was eager to become a nuclear power.

Critics say that Clinton and his lieutenants repeatedly tried to ignore intelligence indicating that Iran was linked to the deadly Khobar Towers bombing in Dhahran, Saudi Arabia in June 1996, which killed nineteen American military personnel. Saudi Hezbollah, an offshoot of the Lebanese-based extremist group backed by Iran, carried out the attack, and it did so with training and logistical support from Iran.

Senior CIA officials played an important role in the Clinton administration's efforts to downplay evidence of Iran's terrorist ties in the late 1990s, according to several CIA sources. In 1996 or 1997, a well-placed officer with the Ministry of Intelligence and Security, Iran's foreign intelligence service, was cooperating with the CIA. In meetings in Europe, just months after the Khobar attack occurred, the Iranian source provided the CIA with evidence that Iran was behind the bombing, according to CIA officials. The Iranian told the CIA he had been meeting with several senior Iranian officials after the bombing, and they were celebrating their successful operation. He also told his CIA contact that sometime after the Khobar bombing, an American government aircraft had secretly landed in Tehran, carrying a senior American official. Several top Iranian officials went out to the airport to meet the American, the source said.

To the officers working on the CIA's Iran Task Force handling the reporting from this Iranian source, it appeared that the Clinton administration was cutting a secret deal with Tehran just after nineteen Americans had been murdered by the same regime. Senior CIA officials responded to this explosive intelligence by suppressing it, according to several CIA sources. According to one CIA source, reports from the Iranian source were delivered to high-ranking CIA officials, but none of the reports was disseminated throughout the intelligence community, and no record of the reports was distributed inside the CIA. It is not known whether President Clinton or other top White House officials were ever told about the reports from the Iranian source. Certainly, then–FBI Director Louis J. Freeh believed that President Clinton and his lieutenants were downplaying intelligence concerning Iran's involvement in Khobar Towers. As he has recently detailed in his memoirs, his anger over the way the Khobar case was handled by the Clinton administration was at the heart of his long-running dispute with the White House. It is not known whether Freeh was ever told about the reports from the source who detailed Iran's role, however.

It wasn't until June 2001, five years after the bombing, and after Clinton had left office, that the Justice Department issued indictments of fourteen people in the Khobar bombing that alleged that unidentified Iranian officials were behind the terrorist attack.

The indictment notwithstanding, in its first few months, the new Bush team largely ignored Iran while obsessing over Iraq. It was only after 9/11 that senior Bush administration officials began to pay attention to low-level, back-channel talks with Iran that had been under way in Geneva since the Clinton days.

Through those Geneva meetings, the Bush team discovered that Iran was strongly supportive of the U.S.-led invasion of Afghanistan because of Tehran's deep hatred for the ruling Taliban, Sunni Muslims heavily dependent on Pakistani support to retain power in Kabul. Shia-dominated Iran long feared the Taliban's radical influence on its own Sunni minority. Tehran also wanted to retain its influence over western Afghanistan, particularly the trading center of Herat.

In 1998, Iran and the Taliban had come close to a shooting war. After nine Iranian diplomats were murdered in Afghanistan and thousands of Shiites were killed following the Taliban seizure of the northern city of Mazar-i-Sharif, Iran massed troops on the border for a military "exercise," and Pakistan had to step in to calm things down. At the time, Iran's leader, Ayatollah Ali Khamenei, made it clear that Iran's patience with the Taliban was wearing thin. "I have so far prevented the lighting of a fire in this region which would be hard to extinguish, but all should know that a very great and wide danger is quite near," he declared, prompting a response from the Taliban that the cleric's statements reflected his "mental ineptitude."

Iran had also supported the opposition Northern Alliance against the Taliban, and after 9/11, Iranian officials at the Geneva meetings were actually impatient with the sluggish start to American military operations in Afghanistan. Publicly, the Iranians said little about the war and provided little overt support to the Americans, apart from promising to allow rescue operations for any downed pilots over its territory. But in Geneva, Iranian officials were eager to help and even brought out maps to try to tell the United States the best targets to bomb.

Iran also held some al Qaeda operatives who tried to flee Afghanistan into Iran. In early 2002, Iran detained about 290 al Qaeda fighters who had been picked up as they crossed the border. They weren't willing to turn them over directly to the United States, but they eventually did hand over some to third countries, such as Egypt, Saudi Arabia, and Pakistan, which were working with the United States.

But by that time, the Bush administration's attitude toward Iran was changing, hardening. Iran was now a member of the "axis of evil." The Iranians responded to Bush's axis of evil speech with pique; Tehran released Gulbuddin Hekmatyar, a ruthless Afghan warlord who had been on the CIA payroll during the 1980s but who was now opposed to the American occupation of Afghanistan. Soon after his release, Hekmatyar's Hezb-i-Islami forces were battling U.S. troops in Afghanistan, and in May 2002 the CIA launched a missile from an armed Predator drone in a vain effort to try to kill him.

The 2003 U.S. invasion of Iraq, on Iran's other border, was met with deep ambivalence in Tehran. The Iranians were happy that the United States was getting rid of their old enemy Saddam Hussein, opening the door for Iraq's majority Shia population to gain power, with, of course, the guidance of Iran. But two consecutive wars in two neighboring countries, first in Afghanistan and now Iraq, had placed thousands of American troops on Iran's exposed flanks, and so it was not hard to see why the Iranians might be getting a little paranoid about the Bush administration's intentions.

In May 2003, one month after the fall of Baghdad, the Iranians approached the United States once again, offering to turn over top al Qaeda lieutenants, including both Saif al-Adel, al Qaeda's chief of operations, and Saad bin Laden, Osama bin Laden's son. This time, the Iranians wanted a trade; in return for the al Qaeda leaders, Tehran wanted the Americans to hand over members of the Mujahedin-e Khalq (MEK), an Iranian exile terrorist organization that had been supported by Saddam Hussein and based in Iraq since 1986. After the fall of Baghdad, the U.S. military had disarmed the MEK's thousands of fighters and taken custody of the group's heavy military equipment, more than two thousand tanks, artillery pieces, armored personnel carriers, and other vehicles provided by Saddam Hussein. But the Bush administration was divided over what to do with the group next.

In a principals committee meeting at the White House in May, the Iranian prisoner exchange proposal was discussed by President Bush and his top advisors. According to people who were in the meeting, President Bush said that he thought it sounded like a good deal, since the MEK was a terrorist organization. After all, the MEK had been a puppet of Saddam Hussein, conducting assassinations and sabotage operations inside Iran from its sanctuary in Iraq. The MEK was officially listed as a foreign terrorist group by the State Department; back in the 1970s, the group had killed several Americans living in Iran, including CIA officers based there during the shah's regime.

Before any exchange could be conducted, the United States would need solid assurances from the Iranians that the MEK members would not be executed or tortured; in the end, that obstacle may have made any such prisoner trade impossible.

But the idea never got that far. Hard-liners at the Pentagon dug in and ultimately torpedoed any talk of an agreement with the Iranians. Defense Secretary Donald Rumsfeld and Deputy Secretary Paul Wolfowitz seemed to think that the MEK could be useful in a future war with Iran, and so they appeared eager to keep the group in place inside Iraq. CIA and State Department officials were stunned that the Pentagon leadership would so openly flaunt their willingness to cut a deal with the MEK; they were even more surprised that Rumsfeld and Wolfowitz paid no price for their actions. At the White House, officials soon learned that the Pentagon was dreaming up excuses to avoid following through on any further actions to rein in the MEK. One argument was that the military was too busy, with too many other responsibilities in Iraq, to devote the manpower to dismantling the MEK. The Pentagon basically told the White House that "we will get around to it when we get around to it," noted one former Bush administration official. "And they got away with it."

The bottom line was that the United States lost a potential opportunity to get its hands on several top al Qaeda operatives, including Osama bin Laden's son. It became clear to frustrated aides that National Security Advisor Condoleezza Rice was not only failing to curb the Pentagon, but was also allowing decision making on Iran policy to drift.

The MEK's political arm, the National Council of Resistance of Iran, understands how to gain attention in the West, particularly after watching the prewar success of the Iraqi National Congress, the Iraqi exile group headed by Ahmed Chalabi. Like Chalabi's group, the Iranian exiles have used the American press to issue claims about Iran's nuclear weapons and ballistic missile programs in order to build the case for a tougher U.S. policy toward Tehran.

While the war in Iraq has overshadowed the issue and forced the Bush administration to move slowly, some administration officials have been advocating a more forceful policy of pressuring the Iranians to disarm. The odds of a confrontation between the United States and Iran seemed to increase in the fall and winter of 2004, when the IAEA reported that Iran was not fully cooperating with international inspectors, and there were new reports that Iran was going ahead with plans to produce enriched uranium despite past assurances to the IAEA that it would freeze such activity. By 2005, Iran's apparent intentions to continue to develop its nuclear program was inevitably leading to a full-fledged diplomatic crisis.

AFTERWORD

I N THE LATE SUMMER of 2005, CIA director Porter Goss received a classified briefing from senior agency officials and analysts that was brutally candid and to the point: the United States was losing the war in Iraq. Two years earlier, when the CIA's Baghdad station chief issued a similarly bleak warning, he quickly discovered that his career was in jeopardy. But in 2005, there were no repercussions for the CIA officers who briefed Goss. Instead, a senior agency official said that he believes Goss's own briefings for President Bush subsequently reflected the agency's downbeat assessment. Sadly, this newfound honesty at the CIA came only after it was already painfully obvious to almost all Americans that the Iraq mission was failing. The CIA's classified assessment could have just as easily come from watching the television news. As the U.S. death toll in Iraq passed the 2,000 mark in the fall of 2005, the Bush administration still lacked a strategy for dealing with the Iraqi insurgency, or even a clear definition of victory. Instead, the White House simply continued to spin the war, arguing that the only two alternatives were Bush's approach or "cut and run." To justify his policies, Bush continued to conflate the fight against al Qaeda with the invasion of Iraq.

To its credit, the CIA issued another classified intelligence assessment in 2005 that could be read as a direct rebuke to Bush's argument that the invasion of Iraq was a critical step in the global war on terror. In the report, the CIA analysts wrote that, far from helping curb terrorism, the war had in fact turned Iraq into a bloody new haven for terrorists, and that it was in Iraq where al Qaeda was enjoying a major revival. Such chaotic conditions did not exist in Iraq before the invasion. Bush's policies had had exactly the opposite of their intended effect. Major newspapers had been reporting similar findings for at least a year. But at least the CIA was no longer so afraid of the White House that obvious, if inconvenient, facts were going unreported in official channels.

The CIA was finally speaking up. Yet no one was listening to the agency or its analysts anymore. The CIA had suffered so many spectacular failures in such rapid succession that by late 2005, it had lost its place and standing in Washington.

The CIA had been so deeply politicized by the Bush administration that its credibility had vanished. If nothing else, the long-running Valerie Plame leak investigation and the indictment of I. Lewis "Scooter" Libby, Vice President Cheney's chief of staff, showed that the CIA had become little more than a political football.

The reforms of 2004 and 2005 that created a new bureaucratic hierarchy for the intelligence community merely papered over the decline and fall of the CIA. The new director of National Intelligence, John Negroponte, was supposed to have broad authority to fix the systematic flaws exposed by both the 9/11 attacks and the inaccurate prewar intelligence on Iraq, but in reality, Negroponte could not compete with the real power in the Bush administration, Donald Rumsfeld.

CIA officials bitterly complained that Rumsfeld and his aides were ignoring the new White House orders and guidelines designed to bolster the DNI's authority to run the intelligence community. Instead, the Defense Secretary seemed determined to bring intelligence within the Pentagon's orbit. The independence of the CIA was slipping away. By late 2005, CIA Director Porter Goss had been relegated to the role of back-bencher, and many of the brightest CIA officers were leaving the agency in frustration.

The CIA had traditionally been the dominant force in the U.S. intelligence community, and that had been by design. When President Harry Truman and Congress crafted the National Security Act of 1947, which established the CIA, one of their goals was to foster a system in which the nation's intelligence service was independent of the military. That was seen as a crucial check on military power. Otherwise, intelligence would be slanted to support the wishes of the general staff. Rumsfeld's power grab is in direct opposition to these goals. It creates one of the most lasting and damaging legacies of the Bush administration: the militarization of American intelligence.

While the CIA had been weakened by five years under George W. Bush, the power of the neoconservatives who had been the agency's most implacable foes has recently begun to wane as well. By the end of 2005, the centerpiece of the neoconservative agenda—Iraq—had turned into the burial ground of their political fortunes.

Championed by Cheney and enabled by Rumsfeld, led by outside advisor Richard Perle and Deputy Defense Secretary Paul Wolfowitz, the neoconservatives had an agenda that was ready made for the world of September 12. They pushed for preemptive war with Iraq and espoused the remaking of the Middle East through the force of American arms. During Bush's first term, they easily swept aside the doubters at the State Department and the CIA, and turned the Pentagon into their policy sanctuary.

The neoconservative rise to power proved to be the most surprising development of the Bush administration, and one that con-

founded and distressed moderates within the Republican establishment. In past GOP administrations, even in the days of conservative icon Ronald Reagan and certainly during the one-term
presidency of Bush's father, Perle, Wolfwitz, and other neocons were
kept on the margins of policy making.

Their stunning rise under George W. Bush deeply divided the
Republican elite in Washington, and many Republican centrists who
served Bush's father came to sound like Democrats as they privately
wondered at the source of the neocon influence over Bush's son. During the 2004 presidential campaign, these Republican moderates for
the most part remained silent. The most noteworthy exception was
Brent Scowcroft, who had served as national security advisor to the
first President Bush, and who inadvertently went public with his
concerns when he gave what he thought was a background interview
to the *Financial Times,* saying that he feared that George W. Bush had
been "mesmerized" by Israeli Prime Minister Ariel Sharon. This followed earlier criticism about the decision to invade Iraq. For his can-
dor, Scowcroft was ostracized by the White House and fired from the
one small assignment he had been given, the chairmanship of the
President's Foreign Intelligence Advisory Board. He has since said,
to *The New Yorker*'s Jeffrey Goldberg, "The real anomaly in the administration is Cheney. I consider Cheney a good friend—I've
known him for thirty years. But Dick Cheney I don't know anymore."

Other disaffected moderates repeatedly predicted the decline and
fall of the neocons, only to watch in dismay as they survived into
Bush's second term. But by late 2005, the neoconservative moment
was ending. Wolfowitz and fellow neoconservative Doug Feith, who
had served as undersecretary for policy, had both left the Pentagon.
John Bolton, a neoconservative at the State Department, was moved
out to the United Nations. With polls showing that the majority of
Americans were turning against the war in Iraq, the neoconserva-

tives and the right-wing pundits who supported them became more defensive, refighting old battles over the war's rationale.

At the height of their power, the neoconservatives had hurled what they considered their greatest insult at the CIA. They said the CIA was filled with "pragmatists" who could only see the Middle East as it was, not as it should be. Dreams die hard, but the dreams of the Bush administration died in places like Fallujah, Ramadi, and Tal Afar.

ACKNOWLEDGMENTS

THIS BOOK would not have been possible without the research assistance of Thomas Risen and Barclay Walsh. I would also like to thank Eric Lichtblau for his reporting help on particularly sensitive issues.

I owe a great debt both to my editor at Free Press, Bruce Nichols, and my agent, Tina Bennett.

Above all, I want to thank the many current and former government officials who cooperated for this book, sometimes at great personal risk.

INDEX

ABOUT THE AUTHOR

JAMES RISEN covers national security for the *New York Times*. He was a member of the team that won the Pulitzer Prize for explanatory reporting in 2002 for coverage of September 11 and terrorism, and he is the coauthor of *Wrath of Angels* and *The Main Enemy: The Inside Story of the CIA's Final Showdown with the KGB*. He lives outside Washington, DC, with his wife and three sons.